PARENTING
through
DIV**O**RCE

PARENTING
through
DIVRCE

Second Edition

*Helping Your Children Thrive During and
After the Split*

LISA RENÉ REYNOLDS, PhD

FOREWORD BY JAMES L. HYER,
ESQUIRE, ATTORNEY AT LAW

Skyhorse Publishing

Skyhorse Publishing books may be purchased in bulk at special discounts for sales promotion, corporate gifts, fund-raising, or educational purposes. Special editions can also be created to specifications. For details, contact the Special Sales Department, Skyhorse Publishing, 307 West 36th Street, 11th Floor, New York, NY 10018 or info@skyhorsepublishing.com.

Skyhorse® and Skyhorse Publishing® are registered trademarks of Skyhorse Publishing, Inc.®, a Delaware corporation.

www.skyhorsepublishing.com

10 9 8 7 6 5 4 3 2 1

Library of Congress Cataloging-in-Publication Data

Reynolds, Lisa Rene.
Parenting through divorce : helping your children thrive during and after the split / Lisa René Reynolds. – Rev. ed.
p. cm.
Previously published under title: Still a family.
Includes bibliographical references and index.
ISBN 978-1-61608-442-4 (pbk. : alk. paper) 1. Children of divorced parents–United States–Psychology. 2. Divorced parents–United States– Psychology. I. Title.
HQ777.5.R49 2011
649'.1–dc23
2011035531

Cover design by Jane Sheppard

Print ISBN: 978-1-5107-2680-2
Ebook ISBN: 978-1-5107-2681-9

Printed in the United States of America

CONTENTS

FOREWORD

President Franklin D. Roosevelt noted, "We may not be able to prepare the future for our children, but we can at least prepare our children for the future." If this book has found its way to you, it is likely that you are facing the prospect of co-parenting following a divorce, and are thus taking a significant step towards preparing your children for their future. As parenting presents significant challenges even when you have a partner offering daily support, the thought of having to parent alone following a divorce can be frightening. The good news is that if approached in a healthy, thoughtful, and organized manner, a divorce may serve as a gateway more so than a roadblock, and afford an opportunity for families to co-parent in a more effectual manner. A useful resource for both lay people and professionals is *Parenting through Divorce*, as Dr. Lisa Rene Reynolds provides a roadmap for parents to make this transition by offering invaluable techniques, insights, and tips during this difficult journey.

I met Dr. Reynolds several years ago when she contacted me regarding the Iona College Marriage and Family Therapy graduate program, where she serves as a professor and director of The Iona Family Therapy Center (IFTC). During my first meeting with Dr. Reynolds, she impressed me with the passion and knowledge she brings to the issues families may endure during the divorce process. Listening to her stories of the clients she has helped over the years, it became clear to me that she is both dedicated to working with her own clients and helping the community through her extensive writing, lecturing, and teaching. Her knowledge and experience have allowed her to assist the individuals she directly serves and a wide range of other people.

After several years of collaborating with Dr. Reynolds, I am pleased that she now has the opportunity to reach an even wider audience and am honored to have been offered the opportunity to write this foreword, as I am confident from my experience as an attorney handling matrimonial and family law matters that this book conveys the much needed information that every parent faced with divorce should have.

The guidance offered in this book is of special importance to me from my perspective as an attorney who has worked with clients on all aspects of divorce, annulment, child custody, visitation, child support, family offense proceedings, and other family law matters. During my initial meeting with every client, educating them on the perils, risks, frustrations, and expense of the litigation process provides them with a glimpse into the realities of an imperfect system. I routinely suggest that the client use the litigation as an opportunity to both prepare for and address the immediate concerns raised in the litigation and, perhaps more importantly, to further plan for the future of their family following the resolution of the litigation. Over the years, I have noticed that most of the clients who take this important advice to heart are often more successful in coping with the significant life transition that occurs following a divorce or a family law proceeding. These clients often come to terms with the fact that they will need to co-parent for the well-being of their children, and also for themselves.

Unfortunately, in my practice, I have also observed clients who remain steadfast in their desire to engage in unnecessary warfare against the other parent to the financial and emotional detriment of their entire family. I recall one case that substantially impacted how I approach cases involving children in family law proceedings, as it provides an illustration of what every reader of this book should strive to avoid for their own family.

When asked to handle a last-minute appearance in the New York City Family Court on an emergency Order to Show Cause seeking to suspend the visitation of my client with his children, I was given little background by the handling attorney and rushed to the courthouse. From the moment of my arrival, the open hostility between my client and his ex-wife was unbe-lievable—shouting in the hallway prior to the appearance, sneering in the courtroom, and a near fist fight after we left. My surprise at the animosity between the parties stemmed not only from the conduct itself, but also due to my review of the motion papers, which revealed that the Order to Show Cause was obviously without any merit. There appeared to be no legitimate reason for these parties to have been in court other than my client's ex-wife using the court system to attack my client without cause. As a young attor-ney, I drove away from the courthouse thinking that the ex-wife was patently unreasonable and felt badly for my client, who I felt was being victimized. Upon returning to my office, I discussed what had occurred with the han-dling attorney who began to laugh. He referred to the client as an "annuity" and offered me the advice that "zebras don't marry elephants." Having repre-sented the client for years, the handling attorney told me that both the client and ex-wife had been battling ferociously in court for years, filing motions every few months against the other. Both were to blame, and all we could do as good attorneys was represent our client's interests to the best of our abilities.

The lesson I learned as a young attorney is pertinent to the subject matter of this book and should serve as a word of caution. Although it may be easy to point to the other person's flaws or mistakes, it is usually harder to identify your own imperfections and errors. Successful co-parenting following divorce requires a commitment by both parents that includes a vigilant dedication to being reasonable and avoiding confrontation with the other parent, even in situations when you believe that you are 100 percent right. Furthermore, this also means you must be willing to admit when you are wrong, identify your own weaknesses and mistakes, and take steps to correct your own behavior. While I believe it is a cynical analogy to say that zebras don't marry elephants, implying that if one party to a marriage has a bad trait, the other party must share that characteristic as well, it is only with cooperation, reasonableness, and willingness to put ego aside in order to reach the mutual goal of familial harmony, and for each side to move on with their lives, that the conflict can properly be resolved.

As I mentioned, I always urge my clients to plan for the future during the divorce process or when they are engaging in any family law proceeding. I stress the importance of utilizing their time and energy to enjoy their lives and to safeguard their limited assets for necessities, such as their children's education. While this may seem untenable during the course of a contentious litigation, it is of the utmost importance to never forget that your life is your own and you make of it what you will. In regard to co-parenting following a divorce, in many cases parents may be successful if they are willing to work for it and avoid unnecessary conflict with the other parent.

Having taken the opportunity to obtain this book, I applaud your efforts to prepare yourself and your family to make effective post-divorce parenting a reality. I also ask that you take into consideration that this endeavor will have a lasting impact upon your children, making your efforts at proper co-parenting one of the most important things you will do. In the words of Frederick Douglass, "It is easier to build strong children than to repair broken men."

—James L Hyer, Esquire, Attorney at
Law – Partner, Bashian & Farber, LLP

INTRODUCTION

It is eight forty-five on a rainy Saturday morning. Twenty-five new faces stare at me from around a large conference table. Some expressions are hard and resentful, others are sad and anxious. There are more than a few people suffering from the pernicious blend of too much crying and too little sleep. Many look curious, wondering what will happen in this room over the next six hours.

This is how the Parent Education Program (PEP) began each week. I taught this six-hour mandatory class for Connecticut parents who were seeking a divorce (or separation if the parents were never legally married) for many years, and it was an integral part of the training and manual revisions. My experience in these classes is why I decided to write this book.

Seventeen states mandate that *all* divorcing parents attend a parenting class, and seventeen more leave the decision to the discretion of the judge. The rest of the states have differing rules on this, most requiring the class only in certain counties or districts (https://www.divorcewriter.com/parent-education-class-divorce.aspx). However, *all* states recognize the growing body of research that supports the many ways that divorce can negatively impact children, and therefore offer elective classes on divorce and parenting.

The six-hour class I facilitated was never quite adequate for addressing all the struggles the participants presented to me. Divorcing parents have so many questions and such a wealth of stories and experience among them; this book focuses on the areas that divorcing parents grapple with most. I address the questions that people asked over and over again in each class. The details may change from family to family, but the core issues are almost always the same among families experiencing a divorce.

The six-hour class I facilitated was never quite adequate for addressing all the struggles the participants presented to me. Divorcing parents have so many questions and such a wealth of stories and experience among them; this book focuses on the areas that divorcing parents grapple with most. I address the questions that people asked over and over again in each class. The details may change from family to family, but the core issues are almost always the same among families experiencing a divorce.

Most people use the old axiom, "About half of all marriages don't make it," as their reference for divorce rates. Indeed, the divorce rate in the United States is most often cited as about 50 percent for first marriages, 67 percent for second marriages, and 74 percent for third marriages. These numbers not only are difficult to accurately gauge, but are probably quite understated. DivorceSource.com is an excellent site for the most cutting-edge statistics on everything divorce. They offer great insight as to why the divorce rate is not always reflected accurately. For example, the divorce rate is based solely on legal, registered marital unions, but does not include any unmarried unions that yield children, such as couples that live together or common-law setups. In fact, the Children's Defense Fund reports that four in ten American children are born to unmarried parents. Additionally, according to the National Center for Health Statistics through the C.D.C., only forty-five states (plus Washington, D.C.) track and report divorce statistics. The data from the remaining states is not incorporated into the national rate.

Every year, more than two million adult Americans divorce. Divorce knows no borders. Couples from various ethnic, religious, and socioeconomic backgrounds go through the ordeal of relationship dissolution. In each of these cases, the littlest victims are the children, and much of the research on children of divorce supports the belief that the process often negatively affects them. There are over one million American children involved in new divorces each year who need their parents to do the right thing.

The changes a divorce brings to a family will be an adjustment for *all* children. Divorce can be devastating for them, but there are many things parents can do to make the experience less traumatic and painful. That's one reason why this book focuses on how the child and the parents experience divorce at the child's various ages and developmental stages. Additionally, the book offers parents practical suggestions as to how to handle common situations with the child and ideas for what to do and how to do it in order to ease the pain of divorce for a child.

No two divorces are the same, and alas, no two families are the same either. For this reason, no step-by-step recipe exists for how to divorce so that children do not suffer. Still, my goal is that this book will help you through each step of your divorce. The stories are real, although I have changed identifying data and specifics in order to protect the identity of the people involved. The suggestions are well-researched, and they are tested in tried-and-true cases by real parents. *I hope you will read this book with great care and hold its message closely; your efforts will go far in helping support your child through this very difficult time.*

1

THE BAD NEWS AND
THE GOOD NEWS . . .
AND HOW TO MAKE
MORE OF THE
GOOD NEWS

The potential negative effects of divorce on children are well documented. Over the years, there have been many research studies on the impact divorce has on children from such well-respected sources as Harvard University Press, the *Journal of Early Adolescence,* the *Journal of the American Academy of Child and Adolescent Psychiatry,* the *Journal of Marriage and the Family,* and the *Journal of Divorce and Remarriage.* The majority of the findings include substantial evidence that children of divorce, as a group, may experience more difficulty in school, more behavioral issues, more social problems, more fighting with parents, more promiscuity, lower self-esteem, and more adjustment issues than children in intact homes. There are also indications that children of divorced parents ("children of divorce") can carry their negative experiences into adulthood, where these experiences can seriously affect their lives and romantic relationships. Adult children of divorce frequently report having commitment difficulties due to memories of their own parents' bad relationships and breakups. These adults may also have poorer communication skills and lower trust levels in their relationships because their own parents did not model those traits.

However, these enhanced risks are generalities and do not speak to any individual child. In fact, numerous studies acknowledge that many children of divorce function just as well as their counterparts. Indeed, some children of divorce may fare even better than children in intact homes, especially when there is chronic violence, fighting, or other dysfunction in the latter. But as a whole, children of divorce are statistically more at risk for several (possibly long-term) problems. By deciding to divorce, parents inevitably increase the chances their children will experience such problems.

Parents in my divorce classes frequently got defensive when we discussed the increased risks for children whose parents divorce. These parents asked, "Aren't the negative effects on kids worse if the parents stay together in a bad marriage than if they divorce?" Certainly, it is not healthy to raise children in a household where parents are continually in conflict or are violent. The negative effects on these children, however, are very different from those that occur when parents choose to divorce. For example, a child from a divorced family may feel abandoned by the parent who has moved out of the house. A child from an intact family with volatile parental interaction will not experience abandonment, but perhaps the child will feel a great deal of stress or nervousness in the home and ultimately anger toward his or her parents.

The bad news is that *all* children of divorce experience some pain and loss from the breakup of their parents' marriage. This is not negotiable or preventable. Even when there may be some sense of relief (as in cases where there was direct abuse, neglect, or continual conflict), children of divorce will have to adjust to the family changes that will unavoidably occur. Feelings of anger, sadness, depression, and confusion are all normal. It's like when a parent puts his or her five-year-old child on the school bus for the very first time. The parent is fully aware that this child will inevitably experience some pain in the school setting. Perhaps there might be an encounter with a bully or the child might be chosen last for a team at recess. Maybe the child will experience rejection by peers or be called a mean name. The parent knows this risk exists on some level, yet he or she smiles and puts the child on the bus anyway because the parent knows that pain is part of life.

In divorce, too, some pain is inescapable, but parents are able to reduce this pain greatly for their children. However, it takes a great deal of commitment and effort from *both* parents. For many divorcing parents, it is just too challenging to parent cooperatively during a time of such anger and conflict, so they fail and their children suffer deeply. Sometimes, one parent will genuinely try to co-parent peacefully but the other parent is too angry, sabotages the attempts, and it turns ugly. Again, the children suffer.

Parents who contemplate divorce do not usually make the decision lightly. They often agonize for many months or even years, wondering what to do. Many parents delay divorce, wondering if they should stay together for the "kids' sake." These parents worry their children might suffer from the divorce. However, the real question is not "Will the divorce affect my child?" but rather "How much will the divorce affect my child?"

The good news is that parents are largely in control of how much divorce will hurt their children. There *are* divorcing parents who successfully communicate and co-parent during and after the divorce, and we can learn from their examples. These parents are able to reduce their children's discomfort and help them see the positive aspects of their "new lives" more quickly.

CASE STUDIES

The following are three examples of parents who have gone above and beyond what is expected of them in order to keep the comfort of their children paramount, even while struggling with the agony of a divorce.

"Bonnie"

Bonnie is a thirty-four-year-old mother of three children, ages five, seven, and eleven. I saw Bonnie and her husband for couples' therapy shortly after Bonnie confronted her husband, "Tim," about cheating on her. Several friends alerted her to frequent sightings of Tim and his girlfriend behaving in an affectionate manner. Tim admitted to having a two-year affair with a woman he worked with and said that he was in love with her. Bonnie was devastated. She filed for divorce two weeks later, and Tim immediately moved in with his lover.

The children remained in the home with Bonnie, and Tim came over frequently to help with homework, yard work, and to take the children to swimming and T-ball practice. The children were very close with their dad and were visibly upset when Tim moved out. Even though he came over often, the children had angry outbursts, cried, and felt a general sadness about their dad's departure.

Soon the time came when Tim said he wanted the children to stay overnight with him at his home with the new girlfriend. The children were unaware of the circumstances that led to the divorce and had no idea that their dad lived with another woman, whom they had never met. Bonnie and Tim sat down with the children and Tim explained that he had a new special friend that he wanted them to meet. He also told them he wanted them to come see the new place where he was living and to stay over for the weekend. The eldest child burst into tears and ran out of the room, and Bonnie suggested that Tim give it some time.

But time did not help the matter. The children refused to go to their dad's new house and said they hated the woman he lived with. Soon the children refused to interact with Tim at all, even in their own home. As hurt and angry as Bonnie was by the whole affair and divorce filing, she knew she had to help her children. And it was not going to be easy.

Later that afternoon, Bonnie gathered the children around the kitchen table, where she had put out chocolate milk and cookies. She met their curious stares with nurturing eyes. Bonnie began: "Listen, guys—we have to talk. I know the last couple of months have been really hard for you, for all of us. I know it hurts, and I know you're angry about some of the changes. But I also know you still love your dad very much. And it's important for you to spend time with him." The youngest child's eyes welled up and his bottom lip quivered a bit. Bonnie fought back tears of her own.

"Your daddy has a person in his life who is very important and special to him. Because this person is so special to Daddy, I think you need to give her a chance. Meet her. You don't have to like her. But I hope you do like her, because then I know it will be much more fun when you go visit Daddy. It's okay if you like her too—it won't hurt my feelings, guys. I think I'd feel relieved. Just give her a chance. It might not be so bad. I know it'll feel weird, but we're all going to have to get used to a lot of weird changes. I know you guys need to spend time with your dad. I can tell you miss him."

Although this monologue was the hardest thing Bonnie ever had to do, in order to ease her children's pain she had to swallow her pride, her disgust for a woman she didn't even know, and her anger toward Tim. Bonnie could see how much the children missed and needed their dad. They didn't need to know about the affair or how Bonnie felt about Tim. But they did need to know that they wouldn't be disloyal to Bonnie by going with Tim. The children needed access to both parents; the roadblock to this was the children's allegiance to their mother and their feeling that they needed to protect her.

The idea of a first visit at Tim's new home was difficult for the children. They were initially nervous and resistant about going, but Bonnie stood at the door with them, encouraging them to go and have fun with Daddy. When the kids told her they felt bad leaving her alone, she smiled and said, "I will miss you very much but I know you'll be having a good time. And I have a lot of work around the house to catch up on, so when you guys get home tomorrow, the work will be done and we can relax and play and you can tell me all about your visit." Bonnie waved and kept that smile on just until Tim's car (with the children buckled safely in back) pulled away. Then she closed the door, slumped down to the floor, and cried.

"Rich and Lynne"

I counseled Rich and Lynne on parenting issues related to their impending divorce. They had two sons together, ages five and nine. They had separated a few weeks before they (mutually) filed for divorce. Rich moved in with his divorced sister and her two kids in a condo that was an hour and a half away from Lynne and the boys. Due to the long commute to Lynne's home and his limited schedule (after picking up a second job to make ends meet and to allow Lynne and the boys to stay in their home), Rich only saw the boys every other weekend. For one son, "Luke," this arrangement was just fine. But for the second son, "Gabriel," it was a lousy situation.

The other piece that complicated the scenario for Rich was that he had two other children from a previous relationship. He saw these children on the same weekend that he had his two boys with Lynne. This made for very little one-on-one time for any of his children, and their visits seemed rushed and chaotic.

Gabriel had always been very close with his dad, but Luke had been more of a "mama's boy." Gabriel cried almost every night for his dad and was continually asking, "When will I see Daddy again?" The answer "in two weeks, honey" would bring on even more tears.

One day, while Lynne was venting her frustration to Rich about what to do about Gabriel, Lynne thought of a plan. She asked Rich if on the every other weekend that was hers (the one when Rich did not see the boys at all) he might be able to meet her halfway somewhere so that Gabriel could spend a little time with him. Rich worked until one on Saturday afternoons, so Lynne offered to bring Gabriel to a halfway meeting point at two on those days. From there, Rich would take Gabriel for a couple of hours to run errands. They picked up dry cleaning, did some grocery shopping, picked up lightbulbs at a home improvement store, got the oil changed, and so on. For a special treat, Rich and Gabriel always made a stop at a particular gas station that sold Gabriel's favorite Yoo-hoo drink. While Rich was with Gabriel, Lynne would do some shopping, see a movie, or go bowling alone with Luke. Both children enjoyed their special time alone with one parent, even if it was only for a few short hours.

Although the children thoroughly enjoyed this setup, it was a huge inconvenience for both parents. Lynne interrupted her weekend to do whatever she wanted with the kids in order to make this extra visit happen for Gabriel. She adjusted her schedule to make the forty-five-minute drive and spent extra money on gas and activities for her and Luke while Gabriel was with his dad. Similarly, Rich sacrificed a large part of his limited downtime and extra money for gas and treats in order to help alleviate Gabriel's sadness. The most important part of this arrangement was that the parents compromised and kept focused on their children's needs and best interests.

"Julie and Billy"

Julie and Billy were enrolled in court-mandated therapy with me due to the high level of disagreement and verbal conflict during their initial divorce proceedings. They had been married for two years and had a five-month-old daughter named "Isabella."

At our first session, Julie and Billy jumped right into their fighting with the topic of the moment: Billy's desire to have Isabella overnight. Julie protested, saying that she was still breast-feeding the baby and that it would be traumatic to have Isabella pulled away prematurely from that comfort. Billy countered by saying that he would have his lawyer make the overnights happen because it was his right to have Isabella half the time, including nighttime. Billy suggested it was time for Julie to wean Isabella from nursing anyway. Julie refused, referring to the American Pediatric Association's recommendation to breast-feed babies at least through one year of age.

Billy then suggested that because Julie was able to pump breast milk ahead of time, she could make enough bottles for him to get through the night. He cited the research on the need for fathers to bond with infants from the start and how divorce made that difficult. He was worried that he wouldn't properly bond with Isabella if he wasn't able to participate regularly in all aspects of her care. Julie was concerned that past attempts at expressing breast milk and feeding Isabella with a bottle had failed; the infant had been very hungry and distressed. Both Julie and Billy were correct in their concerns.

Carefully treading, and being sure to validate both parents' concerns, I suggested that maybe we could come up with some sort of compromise that would reduce the adjustment for Isabella but at the same time meet both parents' needs. The couple laughed and agreed for the first time; they both stated that this would be impossible because they were no good at compromising. I begged them to let me take a stab at it. They agreed.

It took the remainder of the session as well as one half of the next to lead the couple to an agreement they could both live with. It was not my decision, but solely theirs. They were able to put down their defenses and come up with a solution only when I kept them focused on what was least upsetting and traumatic for Isabella.

Their plan called for Julie to spend every other Saturday night on the couch at Billy's apartment while he cared for Isabella through the night in a crib in his bedroom. (This lasted until the baby unexpectedly weaned herself four months later.) It began slowly, with Billy bringing Isabella to Julie around 4:00 AM for the middle-of-the-night feeding she still had not given up. Isabella was still refusing bottles. But not long after, Isabella began sleeping through the night and Julie would nurse her only at 7:00 AM, when the baby awoke hungry. A few weeks later, Julie felt comfortable letting Billy take Isabella overnight without her being there. Isabella had adjusted well because her parents sacrificed and compromised to make that adjustment easier.

Julie certainly did not want to be crashing on her ex-husband's couch two nights a month, and Billy most definitely did not want her there either. But both parents agreed because they could see the positive effect their arrangement had on Isabella. This was the beginning of many compromises Julie and Billy were able to make when they remembered to keep their child's best interests as the central focus.

HOW TO AVOID NEGATIVE VERBAL EXCHANGES THAT HURT YOUR CHILDREN

I have had the opportunity to meet many inspirational parents like Bonnie, Rich and Lynne, and Julie and Billy through my work with divorcing families. But I also see the worst-case scenarios. It is through this wide exposure that I have been able to compile a list of ideals divorcing parents should strive for when modeling communication skills for their children.

Using disparaging comments and fighting in front of the children are perhaps the number-one stressors for children of divorce. The following is a template for "best practices" in avoiding negative verbal exchanges and thereby helping children of divorce to feel less pain and adjust more quickly to the changes in their families. A short discussion follows each suggestion.

Don't Fight in Front of the Kids

If communication between parents is tense or bitter, perhaps the best thing you can do is to keep it out of the view/earshot of the children. This can be extraordinarily difficult to do, especially when there is a great deal of emotional fuel.

Even the youngest of children are aware of harsh tones and unkind words exchanged between parents. Children often hear what their parents mutter under their breath or behind closed doors. You need to be extremely careful with what you say to each other and where you say it.

Most parents do not intend to expose their children to arguments. One divorcing couple I was seeing for therapy came to a session with a ten-month-old baby because the sitter cancelled at the last minute. I agreed to see the couple as long as the conversation was constructive and calm. I reserved the right to end the session early if I felt the conversation was negative or heated. Shortly into the session the couple began to argue, and I interrupted to point out the reaction of the child. The baby, who had been happily cruising around the coffee table in the center of the room and mouthing the toy she held in her chubby little hand, had stopped and was standing still. She was fully focused on her parents, directing her gaze back and forth between the two. The parents had momentarily lost track of everything around them and had been consumed by their anger and aggravation with each other. They had literally forgotten she was in the room. How many times had this happened without these parents even being aware of it?

One common intervention in marital counseling is called "date night." A therapist directs a couple to carve out a specific time each week, with rigid rules: The couple must be alone, and the conversation must be about the couple, not about the kids. I like to prescribe this same intervention to parents who are divorcing, with a slightly different twist: The couple must be alone, but the conversation must be about the kids, not the couple. For couples who tend to get a little heated in their discussions, I recommend going out for coffee in a public place rather than being alone together. Most parents, even when feeling angry, will keep their voices down and act appropriately when there are many others around.

Making time to touch base regarding their children's welfare is perhaps even more important when parents are divorcing than when the parents were together. All too often, after the divorce is final, parents get comfortable with parenting separately, move on with their lives, and less and less frequently contact each other regarding these issues.

When all else fails and parents are completely unable to stop fighting in front of the children, there is one last option. The parents may cease all verbal interaction when the children are present and move to communication via e-mail or a notebook. For children, no verbal communication is better than just plain bad communication.

The notebook option is an especially good one. When one parent needs to vent something to the other, he or she writes it down in the notebook. This gives the parent a chance to reread what he or she wrote and tweak it if necessary. The parent can also choose to run the note by a neutral party, such as a friend or family member, for feedback before giving the notebook to the other parent. Then, rather than being put on the spot, the other parent can choose when he or she feels up to dealing with the issue at hand with the other parent. In this way, the parent does not feel confronted or ambushed at a bad moment but can read the note at his or her leisure. Then, he or she can have the same luxury of writing and rereading the response or sharing it with someone else for comment. Of course, this method works only with nonemergency issues. Concerns needing a more rapid response should be sent via e-mail, or in certain urgent situations a parent may need to pick up the phone and make the call to his or her ex-spouse directly.

Keep the Children's Best Interests as the Focal Point in All Discussions

When divorcing parents keep their discussions geared toward what's best for the children, the conversations generally go better. This is because for most parents the love of the children is the one common ground divorced parents have. For many parents, however, it is very difficult to do this. Some parents are so angry or wounded by the separation/divorce that they find it hard to see outside their own pain and keep focused on the kids.

If you are a divorcing parent who is having a very overwhelming time with the divorce, be sure to take the time and effort to take care of yourself first (see chapter 3); this will maximize healthy and effective parenting. Then, try to keep your conversations with the other parent geared toward the children.

Let's say an argument is brewing between you and the other parent about your annoyance with his or her decision not to attend a child's school play. You might recognize this conversation is fruitless and redirect it toward the effect on the child. Perhaps you might say, "Okay, fine. You're not going to little Johnnie's play tonight. So let's talk about how this might affect Johnnie. Who's going to tell him you won't be there? And what should we do if he gets upset about it?"

One divorcing couple I counseled shouted "Bail!" whenever either of them felt their conversation was deteriorating. This was their clue to refocus quickly.

Give Up Control over the Other Parent's Parenting

When a couple divorces, neither parent has control over how the other parent parents. Parenting is a *right*, not a part in a play that someone else wrote. No one is perfect, and each parent will have to make mistakes in order to find his or her own way. Of course, if one parent is neglecting or endangering a child, that's a different story.

Try to keep conversations with the other parent away from criticizing what he or she does differently than you do. Parenting doesn't have to be the same, and chances are that it never will be. Of course, the more consistency between Mom's and Dad's parenting practices, the easier it is for the children, but this holds true for any family, divorced *or* intact. It makes sense that if the children have a reasonable bedtime at Dad's house (that correlates closely to the one that seems to work well at Mom's house), they will not return to Mom's house the next day feeling cranky and irritable from a lack of sleep.

If you feel you must address a parenting difference that affects the children negatively, try to do so in a calm and nonaccusatory manner. Rather than saying, "It is such bullshit that you return these kids to me whiny and grouchy because you let them stay up all night," you might want to say: "Listen, I need to share my thoughts with you on something. I know you have the right to parent however you see fit during your time with the kids, but I feel like they push staying up late at your house and when they don't get enough rest, they suffer the next day. I just wanted to make you aware that some days, I notice they don't seem to have gotten enough rest and maybe you don't notice it because they are back with me by then."

There's no guarantee that reframing your statements and tone will result in having the other parent change or even see your point of view. But the change in your *delivery* of the words will certainly have a more positive influence on the direction and possible outcome of the conversation.

Use "I Statements"

"I statements" are a cornerstone of effective communication. They should replace the opposing "You statements" that imply fault or blame. Some examples of common *you* statements are "You are crazy," "You can't go," and "You are controlling me." I statements that correspond with these same examples might be "What I'm hearing from you doesn't seem like it is well thought out," "I don't feel it's a good idea for you to go," and "I feel like you're not letting me have a say in this matter." So, for example, "You interrupted me," might be replaced with the I statement, "I am feeling like you don't want to listen to me about this."

I statements are helpful in avoiding assumptions, and when you use them, you are never wrong. This is because when using I statements, you are speaking only about what you feel and believe to be true. You are entitled to your own beliefs. They may be challenged by the other parent (that's what happens in communication), but your feelings cannot be denied.

I statements can be helpful in facilitating more peaceful communication between parents in disagreement or conflict. Using them also sets an excellent example for children and can reduce the fighting they are exposed to.

Be Flexible

Life is not a pretty picture that hangs on the wall and never changes. Flexibility is a necessary part of living; when parents are prepared to bend a little, it makes life's unexpected twists and turns more bearable.

One parent may attempt to control the other parent or take advantage of him or her by continually asking for changes to the parenting plan to suit that parent's needs. This is a blunt misuse of the flexible co-parenting arrangement and is not acceptable. However, it is helpful when divorcing parents can be less than rigid when dealing with the occasional unexpected change requested by the other parent. For example, let's say you ask to swap weekends with your husband or wife because there's a family reunion you'd like to attend with the kids. If he or she doesn't already have an equally important commitment, that parent should make the effort to accommodate this arrangement. Likewise, if he or she asks to pick the kids up a couple of hours later than usual one Friday due to mandatory training at work, you should try to make this work.

Remember to Mention the Good Stuff

One of the biggest tension triggers for divorcing parents is when one parent continually criticizes the other. Snide remarks and sarcasm will not create an environment for peaceful communication. As one of my divorced therapy clients put it: "It doesn't feel good to have my ex continually point out all my flaws and weaknesses. I can only hear so much of how inadequate I was in bed or how much weight I've gained or how our daughter hates me before I completely shut down or lose it on her."

Try to remember that even though you may be divorcing, you must remain co-parents for the rest of your lives. In order to nourish this necessary relationship with your ex-spouse, a little "good stuff" goes a long way. Try to focus on the positive things you see, as difficult as it may be during such an emotional and trying time. Perhaps an ex-spouse has made an excellent effort to attend all the children's school activities and sports events. You might point out to him or her that you valued the effort.

A divorced client I once saw for treatment told me that amid a very bitter divorce, the nicest and most meaningful thing his ex-wife ever said to him was that she appreciated him being timely with the child-support checks. He reported that because his ex-wife said that to him, he softened a bit toward her and made every effort to ensure that all the other financial stuff was done when it was due. Don't people like to hear that their positive efforts have not gone unnoticed?

*   *   *

Remember that there is more than loss and sadness that children can experience from a divorce. An important gift children can receive from the divorce is a model for good behavior and respect between their parents.

2

REDUCING THE RISK OF TRAUMATIZING YOUR CHILDREN

Parents report the initial decision to divorce as one of the most diffi-cult, heart-wrenching choices they ever have to make. In fact, many parents delay the decision to divorce for many months, even years, because they don't want to hurt their children. Inevitably, though, one parent reaches the breaking point and decides to end the marriage.

The vast majority of divorces are initiated by one partner. Rarely do both parents sit down over dinner one night and say in unison, "Gee, honey, I was thinking that things are not good between us and haven't been for a long time and maybe we should break up." This extremely atyp-ical scenario might be followed by one parent suggesting, "Okay, dear, let's grab the phone book and choose a divorce lawyer to contact in the morn-ing," and the other parent responding with a resounding, "Sounds great!"

In the real world, one parent is the "ender" and the other parent is the "endee." Even if both parents have been unhappy and are toying with the idea of divorce, there is usually only one who really "ends" the marriage. This can often set up one parent as being "the bad guy" and the other as being "the victim." This can create a lack of balance in what remains of the marital relationship, sometimes causing a whole host of issues between parents. But the principal victims are often the children.

So what can parents do from the very beginning to reduce the risk that the decision to divorce will traumatize their children? First and foremost, they need to take care of themselves mentally, physically, and emotionally. (See chapter 3 for more on this important topic.)

HOW TO TELL YOUR CHILDREN ABOUT THE DIVORCE

Before telling your children about your impending divorce, you need to determine who will tell them, when you will tell them, and what you will tell them. Preparation is the key. Arrange a time to discuss your plans with each other (*at least* once) prior to meeting with your children. The goal is to avoid either parent being surprised by what the other might say. This also allows each parent to point out things the other may not have thought of. Some parents I see for therapy report that running their comments by a third, unbiased party has been helpful as well in getting feedback before they talk to the children.

Parents should make a few other preparations before talking with the kids. Reduce distractions before you begin (turn off cell phones and any other electronic devices). Make the setting as comfortable as possible (adjust the thermostat if necessary, clear off chairs and couches, make younger children's favorite blankets or stuffed animals available).

Who Should Tell the Children
If at all possible, *both* parents should tell the children about the divorce, even if one of you is afraid of being emotional or doesn't want the divorce. This presents a united front to the children and lets them know that everyone has heard the same information.

Some emotion or crying from parents is normal and expected. You need not worry about hiding sadness from your children. In fact, showing some disappointment or sadness may validate any feelings your children may be experiencing.

In rare cases, one parent may not be present to tell the children about the divorce. Perhaps the parent is incarcerated, has moved out of the state, or is in a treatment facility. In these situations, one parent may have to break the news to the kids alone. *This parent needs to be very careful to remain neutral and not blame or criticize the absent parent.*

Occasionally, there are other reasons one parent may not be available to speak with the kids about the divorce. Some parents will not acknowledge the end of the marriage and therefore refuse to participate in telling the children. Others are too angry and volatile to be included in the discussion with children.

Most important, you need to make sure that someone outside the family does not leak the news of divorce to the children before you have the chance to talk to them about it. *Be clear to others that they are not to speak to the children about the divorce before you have had an opportunity to speak with them about your decision.*

When to Tell the Children

Tell the children about the divorce *before* any major changes occur in your family (like one parent moving out or selling the family home), but *after* the decision to divorce is certain. There's not much worse than putting children through the news of their parents' divorce only to retract the decision a few days later. Of course, unexpected reconciliations do occasionally occur. Still, the rule of thumb is *not* to share the news with your children until you have a firm decision and will be filing for divorce imminently.

Timing is of utmost importance when telling children of an impending divorce. It's important to select a time when your children are not overtired or irritable. Avoid doing it at the end of the day or for younger children just before naptime. Also avoid approaching the children when they may be hungry. Make sure they have had a snack or meal before having the conversation.

It's also important to choose an occasion where there are no time constraints (like needing to run off to work or school right afterward). There should be ample time for discussion or questions the children may ask. There should be time and flexibility as well for follow-up on any promises you make to your children. For example, if you say you will keep the kids updated on all the changes that will be happening, it is important to follow through on that. In a discussion about new living arrangements, for example, maybe you both could follow up by taking the children to see the new apartment one of you will be living in and then taking them out for ice cream afterward.

Keep in mind that more than one discussion about the divorce will be necessary. Many times, the initial conversation is the most difficult. Subsequent chats may seem a bit easier. However, many parents get the first conversation over and done with and then think they're out of the woods. This is generally not the case. As the information you share with your children begins to sink in, more thoughts and questions may surface. Also, the process of separation and divorce brings wave after wave of change for families. As each change occurs, children may develop new concerns that parents need to address. It's wise to plan on having many conversations about your divorce over these growing years. The questions a five-year-old may have will certainly be different from the ones a child of nine or fourteen will want to ask.

Where to Tell the Children
Parents should talk to their children in the comfort of their own home. However, they should also think through which actual *space* they use within the home.

Parents should choose a neutral space (like a living room, kitchen, or study). Never choose a child's bedroom, because he or she may forever link this traumatic memory to his or her sleeping space. The parents' bedroom (or a spare room where a mom or dad had been sleeping apart from the other parent) is also not a good choice. These settings may highlight the loss of one parent more so than in a neutral site.

Also, parents should be careful to select a safe spot in the home (if at all possible). For example, if a child gets very upset or angry and runs out of the room, be certain there are not bulky items in the hallway that the child could trip over. Likewise, parents should be cautious of telling their children about the divorce in a place that is very close to a steep set of stairs or a wide-open window.

What to Tell the Children
Think carefully about what you want to say and how you want to say it beforehand. Be prepared to offer your children some detail on what the divorce will mean for the family. Simply saying, "We're getting a divorce," is meaningless unless some explanation follows. They will want to know what changes will happen and how the divorce will affect their lives. Common questions include "Will we still live here?"; "Who will we live with?"; "How often will we see each parent?"; and "Will we have to change schools?"

Be straightforward with what you tell the children about the divorce. Use simple terminology and clear terms: "Mommy and Daddy are going to get a divorce. What this means is that Mommy and Daddy are not going to be married anymore and we will live in separate homes." For younger children, using the word *divorce* may not even be necessary. However, I find that more and more young children are aware of the word and know fully its meaning. This is most likely due to the growing number of marriages that fail early on when children are still very small. In fact, young children in general (even those from homes with happily intact parental units) worry about divorce when they hear their parents have a simple argument about something. This speaks to the level of fear children have about this dreaded "D word."

Limit your discussion to a few main and urgent issues when telling your children about the divorce. Children can become overwhelmed and confused if they receive too much information. You can add detail as a child requests it or after you have given the child some time to think about the initial news of divorce.

Remember also that *telling* children about the divorce is not a be-all and end-all; an important part of giving children the news of a divorce is *listening* to what they have to say in response. You need to hear your children's thoughts and concerns about the divorce and give them a chance to ask questions or get clarification on certain issues.

Many parents feel pressured into answering every question their children have, and they struggle with how or what to say in response. *It is not mandatory to address or answer every question.* For example, if a child asks an inappropriate or embarrassing question of Mom or Dad, that parent has the right to refrain from answering. The parent might explain to the child that the question is of a personal and adult nature and that he or she is uncomfortable discussing that information with the child.

You should also be careful not to disclose personal information about the other parent. For instance, let's say a child asks Dad why Mom didn't come home last night and where she was. It would not be advisable for Dad to offer that Mom got fired from her job, went out and got drunk, and ended up calling to say she was sleeping over at her new boyfriend's house. A better alternative might be for Dad to say, "I think those are questions you need to talk to your mom about. I don't really want to speak for her."

One woman I saw for treatment offered an excellent example of why divorcing parents should sometimes refrain from answering *every* question in full detail.

"Carly" was in her midthirties when she came to me for therapy. She had recently ended a relationship with a man she described as "yet another loser." She was concerned about her recent string of failed romantic relationships and why she made such poor choices in men. She offered me a thumbnail sketch of her life, focusing a great deal on her parents' volatile divorce when she was fourteen. Carly described her father as a "lying, cheating bastard" and her mother as a "victim."

She recounted the day her mother sat her down to tell her she was leaving Carly's father.

> She [Carly's mother] had been crying. I could see her hand shaking as she clutched her morning mug of coffee. My father had not come home the night before. The house was silent except for her occasional sniffle. She came right out and said it—she was going to divorce my father. I have never been as angry as I was on that day. I started screaming at my mother. I yelled at her for putting up with his shit and letting him get away with lying and not coming home and I told her it was about time she got rid of him. I said I wished he would never come home and that he'd be better off dead. I asked my mother directly—he's cheated on you, hasn't he? She nodded. I asked her how many times and with how many different women. She answered me—"Countless times with at least seven women I know of." I asked her if we knew any of the women. She nodded again and mentioned the name of a neighbor. I told my mother I knew that she wasn't having sex with my father because he was never home and if he was, he slept on the couch. She nodded. "How could he do this to you?" I cried out. "You deserve better!"

Carly went on to tell me that her mother had not really told her anything she had not already known on some level. Looking back, she even knew there had been more than just a friendly relationship between her father and the neighbor. However, her mother's willingness to confirm the awful details of her father's behavior only seemed to back up Carly's role in having to take a stand on this.

Carly told me she wished her mother had done things differently. When I asked her how, this is what she replied:

> I wish she hadn't actually answered my questions. I already knew the answers to what I was asking, but the reason I was asking, I think, was to get ammunition against my father. After she confirmed what he had done, I was even more horrified and built up a huge wall of resentment for him. To this day, I cannot get the image of my father caressing the neighbor's back out of my head. I find myself wondering if he ever had sex with one of these women right there on our living room couch. I thought of him panting and groaning and then I couldn't ever stop hating him.
>
> Sometimes I wish my mother would have just said, "Carly, there are lots of hard things to deal with in grown-up relationships. The details don't matter. What matters is that I'm not happy and your father and I have a relationship that isn't working. I've tried to figure this out for a long time and this is what I need to do now. I'm scared but I know it's what I have to do."

Carly ended the session by saying to me, "Maybe I could have more easily moved past all this if my mother had given me permission to not be bothered with it. Maybe if she had let me know not to worry about it and that she had control and knew what she was doing, I could have let it go. And maybe that's why I cannot forgive any of the men I date."

One important rule of thumb to remember is that when children ask questions, they ask because they want to know *how* the answers will affect them. If the child asks, "Will Dad be moving out of the house?" what he or she really wants to know is *when* Daddy will go, *when* the child will see Daddy, *where* he will live, and perhaps if a pet will be allowed there. Keep this in mind and answer your child's (seemingly basic) questions accordingly.

In addition to telling the children about your impending divorce and answering their basic questions, you should be ready to assure your children of two very important things. First and foremost, children need to hear that their parents love them and always will, no matter what changes happen in the family. You need to both say this and show it through your actions (see chapters 7, 8, and 9 for specific ideas on how to show love in creative ways to children in different age groups).

Even if staying away from the family or spouse seems less painful for one parent, he or she needs to stay engaged with the children and see them frequently. And buying things doesn't count—parents cannot replace or substitute love and quality time with toys or treats.

During the tender first days of hearing the news of divorce, children need their parents to be present and accessible. You should plan on a lot of downtime around the home for a few days if at all possible to reinforce that message of availability.

Second, it's important to remember to tell your children (sometimes over and over again) that they are not responsible for the divorce. And even then, telling children this doesn't guarantee they'll believe it! Many children blame themselves for the divorce or at the very least feel that if they could have been "better," maybe it would have helped the parents stay together.

I once saw a six-year-old boy for therapy regarding his adjustment to his parents' disagreeable divorce. He looked at me boldly and said he knew how to fix his parents. He stated that he was sorry for being so bad and was going to be nicer to his sister, not tease the dog anymore, and would pick up his room. "Then they won't fight anymore and won't get divorced," he said matter-of-factly. As hard as his parents tried to convince him that he wasn't the cause of the divorce, this little boy remembered his parents disagreeing over how to deal with his messy room and his fighting with his sister, and he was certain that his past actions caused distress that ultimately led his parents to divorce.

In the case where a child thinks he or she was responsible for the parents' breakup, it's so important that parents refrain from arguing in front of that child. Additionally, *both* parents should be careful in how they address and discipline the child when he is arguing with his sister or is not cleaning his room. And *both* parents need to continue to let the child know it's not his fault.

Children also need to know that the divorce is final. Many children overestimate their power in influencing their parents' relationship. It can be useful to say, "The decision to divorce was *ours* and you neither have the power to cause our problems nor to fix them."

It is also common for children to wish for their parents to get back together. Children easily misconstrue things as signs that their parents may reconcile. This happens more frequently in families where the divorcing parents have a very friendly, respectful relationship and children don't understand why their parents are splitting up.

A nine-year-old boy once said to me in therapy, "I don't get it—why are my parents divorcing? We all have dinner together a couple of times a week, everyone gets along fine, we went to Disney World last year; we even have season box seats to all the Yankees games." Clear messages that center on the fact that the divorce is certain, regardless of how sad it may be for the children, are imperative. The following is an excerpt from a session I had with two distraught, divorcing parents shortly after they told their children about their decision to divorce. It demonstrates the power of young children's wishful thinking and the importance of clear messages.

The "Carr" family consisted of the mother ("Annie"), the father ("Sean"), and twin five-year-old boys ("Finn" and "Ryan"). Annie and Sean had separated a few months prior to my initial meeting with them and their boys. Sean had recently moved into an apartment nearby and Annie retained the primary residence with the boys. Annie and Sean reported the boys had been "very sad" about the news that their parents were getting a divorce.

It was the first Christmas the boys would not spend with both parents at the same time. The plan was for Sean to see the boys for a while on Christmas Eve and then turn them back to Annie by 8:00 PM. Annie would spend Christmas morning at home with the boys and then drive to upstate New York to spend a few days with the twins and her family.

Annie and Sean had maintained a respectful and polite relationship throughout the divorce proceedings, so Annie was comfortable having Sean come to her home to spend time with the boys on Christmas Eve. Annie stayed "in the background," busying herself upstairs so that Sean could have some undivided, quality time with the twins.

Sean and the boys hung stockings, baked cookies, hung tinsel, and read many holiday books together snuggled up by a blazing fire. Soon, eight o'clock came and Sean noticed it had begun to snow pretty heavily. He told the twins that he needed to get going and that they needed to get to bed if they wanted Santa to come. After many little pleas from Finn and Ryan, Sean laid out carrots for the reindeer, put out the fire, put the angel on top of the tree, and tucked the boys in with the proverbial visions of sugarplums. He hurried downstairs to leave for home.

Annie watched from the front door as Sean's car tires slipped and spun; he was ultimately unable to get the car up the driveway. Annie ran out to try to help shovel a bit but it was no use; Sean was stuck. Suddenly, two little smiling heads peeked out from around the front door that Annie had left ajar. Finn and Ryan were shrieking, "Can Daddy stay? Can he, can he please?"

Sean and Annie exchanged awkward looks and then Annie nodded and said, "I don't think we have a choice, boys. I guess Daddy's going to have to camp out on the couch." "I hope Santa doesn't mind me there," Sean added, with a hearty laugh.

Sean slept on the couch that night and indeed, Santa had arrived by morning. The boys awoke to a tree full of gifts, overflowing stockings, a beautiful breakfast spread that included Annie's homemade cinnamon rolls, and several hours of family fun.

By eleven o'clock the festivities were done. Sean gathered up his things and told the boys the roads were clear and he was going to head home. The boys begged him not to go. Sean replied, "But kids, you guys have to head up to Grandma and Grampy's house soon. You get to see your Aunt Sarah and all your cousins and I bet Santa may have left a little something for you up there too." The boys continued to beg and cry and soon it became a full-blown meltdown. This unhappiness lasted for several days.

Annie and Sean called me three days after Christmas, asking for an "emergency" appointment to process what had happened. They all felt awful about how the first holiday apart had turned out. When I met with Sean and Annie, their first response was agreeing that they "never should have let Sean stay over." I challenged their thought with, "Why not?" They replied, "Because the boys thought that Daddy sleeping over meant we were all going to be a family again."

I initially confirmed how difficult it was for the children to accept their parents' divorce and the sad changes it brought to their family. I also reminded Sean and Annie of two things. First, it was not a bad thing to have looked out for the safety of a family member they cared about. The travel conditions were treacherous, and had it been any family member other than Sean out there, the parents would not have hesitated to invite the person to crash on the couch for the night.

Second, there was simply no choice in the matter; Sean was stuck and had to spend the night. Through some discussion around these themes, Sean and Annie were able to see that their mistake had not been in letting Sean spend the night. Rather, their mistake had been in not telling the boys that Daddy spending the night did not mean the family would always be together in that manner; the family would not spend future Christmases together in this way. Initially, Sean and Annie felt that it would have been cruel to have said those words to the boys on Christmas Eve. I pointed out that perhaps it would have been crueler to let the boys spend all Christmas Eve and Christmas morning believing their family was back together forever, and then seventeen hours later springing it on them that this was not the case. The Carrs agreed.

ONCE YOU'VE TOLD YOUR CHILDREN ABOUT THE DIVORCE

Perhaps even more important than what and how parents tell their children about the divorce is how they support the children afterward. The following are some guidelines for helping children best adjust to the changes a divorce will bring in the early days.

Accept Initial Reactions
There are many normal ways a child may react to the news of a divorce in his or her family. Some children may appear shocked and others may report they weren't at all surprised. Some children will be outwardly emotional (yelling or crying) but others may hold it in, becoming distant or quiet. A few children may even remain in denial about what they were told and may not seem to have any initial response at all.

Accept all reactions. There is no right or wrong way for a child to respond to such serious news. Furthermore, there are no right or wrong feelings to have when a child hears of the divorce. Common feelings include anger, sadness, confusion, hurt, loneliness, self-blame, worry, powerlessness, rejection, and—*in very few cases*—relief. It may help to think for a moment about your own range of feelings about the divorce. Most divorcing parents admit that some days they wake up feeling empowered and sure they've made the right decision, but on other days they may be consumed by sadness and doubt about whether they are doing the right thing.

In short, there is a wide range of common emotions and reactions that children may experience when parents initially tell them about the divorce; *all* of them are normal and okay. If children's responses seem persistent or worrisome, please see chapters 7, 8, and 9 on individual age groups for a more detailed discussion on when to be concerned and how to address children's reactions to divorce.

Help Your Kids Deal with Their Feelings

There are many ways that people in general express and deal with negative emotion. Children are no different. However, with such limited life experience, many children will require help in learning what to do with such feelings.

First, it's important to be direct in saying that whatever your child is feeling is acceptable. "It's okay to feel angry," sends an important message to children that it's valid to feel a certain way.

Also, never criticize your child for experiencing any emotion. If your child cries and expresses hatred toward you or your spouse for "ruining my life," you need to be sensitive to the child's experience. In this scenario, a nonsupportive response would be: "Oh, c'mon now, you don't really hate us. No more tears now. It's not so bad. There are many worse parents you could have." A better reply might be: "Wow—that's a really strong feeling to have. But it's okay—believe it or not, we understand and know you need time to understand this. We're sorry you have to go through this and wish there was something we could do to change how you feel about it."

During the process of divorce, expressing negative emotion is an integral part of the healing process. And although *all* feelings are valid, not *all* ways of expressing these feelings are acceptable or desirable. You can play a key part in helping your children to learn healthy ways to vent emotions such as anger and frustration.

There are ways that assist both "stuffers" (children who hold all their emotions inside) and "exploders" (children who act out their emotions in undesirable ways, such as hitting or breaking things) with expressing feelings. The rule of thumb should be *not* to change the feeling your child is having, but rather to find an appropriate outlet for the emotion in order to help the child better cope with it.

Talking is not always the preferable mode of dealing with emotion for children (especially very young ones). Help your children channel the emotional energy into something; doing and playing can often yield much better results. The following is an example of how play elicited far more information than talking could have with a very young child I saw for therapy.

"James" was a two-year-old boy whom the court mandated to attend a few therapy sessions with me after he exhibited a great deal of anger; namely, hitting and biting his parents and other children at his day care. His parents said the behavior started when they began their (very nasty) divorce proceedings. Each parent blamed the other for James's escalating behavior.

I questioned how effective a few sessions with James would be given that his verbal abilities were extremely limited. Nevertheless, I jumped into some traditional play therapy with him, hoping to get some understanding of what he was thinking or feeling.

Together, we tackled a huge mound of wooden blocks. We built for a few minutes in silence and then decided our creation looked like a castle. I put a moat around the castle and explained its purpose to James. Then I let him choose whether the moat should be filled with alligators or sharks. He chose sharks.

I used some items from around the room to represent James's family members. James chose a black marker for his dad, a silver car key for his mom, a tiny plastic duck for himself, and various other objects for his stepbrother, grandparents, and Aunt Judy. I placed "Dad" (the black marker) on top of the castle. Then I put "Mom" (the car key) on the wall of the moat. I asked James if that looked right to him. He grabbed a spare block and hit "Dad" off of the castle. Then he went over to retrieve "Dad" and used him to knock "Mom" into the "waters" of the moat.

I was getting a great deal of information from James, so I decided to continue on with our castle play. By the end of my thirty-five minutes with him I had a pretty good understanding of the family dynamics as James saw them. I learned that Dad was not the desirable leader of the family, that Dad did not allow Mom anywhere inside the walls surrounding the castle, that James hid himself beneath blocks whenever possible, and that Mom never came over to uncover James. I received far more knowledge on where James's anger stemmed from than I ever could have extracted with words or questions alone.

Outdoor physical play, shooting hoops, digging, and dancing are great outlets for children (and many adults as well). Less physically active play and creative activities can be helpful coping mechanisms for children as well. You can encourage your children to transfer their feelings into artwork ("Can you draw me a picture of how you feel?" or "What colors do you think you'd use to color in this picture of our house today?"). The simple use of finger paint or Play-Doh can be therapeutic (if you haven't ever done it as an adult, you should give it a try). You can also encourage your children to keep a diary. This is an especially effective tool for dealing with emotions. Another benefit of the journaling is that as time goes by, your children can look back over past entries and see the changes they have made in their thoughts and feelings.

Remember that parents are one of the primary role models their children have for how to express negative emotions in meaningful ways. As the old adage goes, "Children learn as they live." Perhaps the most powerful tool that you as divorcing parents have in helping your children is to offer tangible examples of how to vent emotions appropriately. If you use such coping skills as talking to a friend, praying, seeing a therapist, screaming into a pillow, writing in a journal, or going for a run, you should share these things with your children.

Lean on Friends and Family (and Even Your Ex-Spouse)

Many parents are surprised to learn that loneliness is something many children of divorce experience. During and after divorce, parenting time is usually with *one parent at a time.* That means one parent is responsible for everything—working, cleaning, cooking, homework, laundry, baths, bedtime—during his or her time with the children. This is particularly difficult if there is more than one child. Without a second set of hands to help out, a parent may find it challenging to be available for each child's needs. A parent may feel "spread thin," and the children may feel needy for their parent's time and attention.

When you are feeling overwhelmed (or if it seems there is not enough time in the day to complete all that must be done), it may be helpful to lean a bit on family and friends. Asking for help is hard for many parents, especially when they want to prove to themselves they can do it all on their own after the divorce. Yet assistance from others can be a huge benefit to both the parent *and* the children. Involvement with aunts, uncles, grandparents, and cousins can help your children stave off feelings of loneliness. You may find comfort in knowing the children are safe and being cared for by someone who perhaps has a bit more time and energy to offer them.

One divorcing Mom I saw for therapy said that the most important thing she ever did for herself and her kids was to ask her sister for an entire day of babysitting so that she could catch up on some much-needed housework. The mom's sister took the kids to the park, a museum, out to lunch, and back to her house to do artwork and play some board games. In this scenario, everybody was a winner; the sister felt good about finally knowing how she could help, the kids came home happy but exhausted from the fun day, and Mom caught up on her cleaning so she had time to relax with her children upon their return.

Some divorcing parents (if they are amicable) may consider asking each other for help when they feel overwhelmed. Occasionally accommodating the other parent and his or her needs will benefit your children in a sense as well: A healthy, well-rested parent is more able to parent effectively.

One divorcing couple I saw in counseling agreed to tweak its parenting plan a bit in order to be of service to each other and to increase the attention each child received from each parent. Rather than the typical every-other-weekend-with-one-parent scenario, these parents decided on this monthly schedule: One weekend both kids were with Mom, the next weekend both kids were with Dad, the next weekend one child was with Mom (the other child was with Dad), and the last weekend the children swapped and the child who had been with Mom was now with Dad (and vice versa). This arrangement gave the two children ample time alone with Mom and Dad. Unfortunately, though, what was best for the children also left both Mom and Dad with only one weekend a month with no children at all. This took a toll on the availability of "me time" for both parents and reduced the time the parents could spend with their new significant others. To alleviate this strain, each parent allowed the other parent two "swap days/nights" per month. This meant that if Dad was available to take the kids on a Monday afternoon and night that was normally Mom's parenting time, Mom could ask to use one of her "swaps" so that she could have dinner with friends, come home late, and sleep in a bit the next day. Both Mom and Dad found their parenting agreement to work quite well across the board.

Consider Contacting Other Important People
When parents decide to divorce, they sometimes forget to inform certain (important) parties about the changes that will be soon occurring. Most parents tell family and close friends about the split, but there may be others who would benefit knowing about the divorce.

For example, if you are going through a bitter divorce, talk to your boss or a couple of trusted coworkers about what's going on. This disclosure will give them much-needed information about why you may occasionally be late to work, show up with puffy eyes from crying, or need to leave work early one day for a court date. Most bosses and coworkers will cut an employee a little slack if they know the worker is temporarily going through some difficult personal issues.

You may also consider telling a few neighbors or more distant friends in order to avoid an uncomfortable situation later. Many divorcing parents have told me there is little worse than having unknowing neighbors unexpectedly ask why they haven't seen the ex-spouse around lately. This can be especially difficult if the neighbor asks while the children are within earshot and a quick explanation is necessary.

In addition, you can increase your children's support and comfort by addressing the divorce and subsequent family changes with other care providers. It may be helpful to inform day care workers and schoolteachers that your family is going through a divorce. Teachers will not typically contact a parent about a child unless a certain behavior becomes clearly troublesome. However, a parent can tell the school to be on the lookout for any subtle behavior changes a child may exhibit during the divorce. The earlier the school can let a parent know of any concerns about a child, the sooner the parent can address the problem or get help for it.

Don't Be a Cheerleader
One mistake divorcing parents frequently make is in trying too hard to be cheerleaders about the eventual benefits of the divorce. Helping your child hear and digest the news of a divorce includes understanding that he or she may not agree that a divorce is desirable. In fact, *the vast majority of all children whose parents divorce wish their parents would stay together.*

You need to acknowledge that even if you think your divorce is for the best, your children will most likely not agree. Reflect this acknowledgment in the way you respond to your children. For instance, if your child declares his or her unhappiness about your divorce, you should never try to convince that child that happiness is required.

The best (and only) way to convince a child that the divorce is for the best is to give it some time and show the child a healthier and happier family system postdivorce. Think about it: If you tell your children that the forkful of a new slimy green vegetable tastes really, really good, they probably won't believe you just because you said so. But if your child is brave enough to take a bite and discovers the veggie tastes just like cotton candy, he or she will be a believer!

*   *   *

From the very beginning, there are many things parents can do to help their children cope with divorce. Remember that these guidelines are meant to support a best-case scenario. Try to stick to them as much as possible to reduce the amount of stress and anxiety your child will experience when he or she hears the news of the divorce. Still, no one is perfect, and sometimes people make mistakes. If you find yourself "messing up" (e.g., yelling at your spouse, making a snide comment), just try to refocus and work harder. At the very least, when you've cooled off, you should be sure to show your children that you take responsibility for your errors ("I shouldn't have said what I said"), tell them why your behavior was wrong ("It was not nice or respectful"), why you did what you did ("I got angry and lost my temper"), and what you're going to do about it ("I will have to work on better ways to handle my anger"). The effort to minimize stress on children in the beginning stages of divorce can be hugely successful.

3

Taking Care of Yourself . . . for Your Kids

Although the process of divorce takes a toll on *everyone* in the family, sometimes parents can be hardest hit. The financial and legal pressures of divorce and the subsequent demands of single parenting can create a great deal of stress, which can reduce a parent's patience and good judgment. Perhaps the most important thing parents can do to support their children during the divorce is to take care of *themselves* first so that they will have the energy and focus to parent effectively.

It may seem obvious that a well-rested, emotionally stable parent is better able to find the patience and emotional availability his or her children need during the divorce process. Yet many parents fail to care for their own physical and emotional needs properly during this difficult time. As a result, children of divorce often suffer unnecessarily.

Many parents report not sleeping or eating well, smoking or drinking too much, or feeling depressed during their divorce proceedings. These are factors that can increase a parent's irritability and lack of patience; decrease the parent's energy, interest, or involvement with his or her children; and often result in poor parent-child interactions.

Almost all divorcing parents insist they want to "stay strong" for their children and be supportive of them during this time of sadness and change. *Parents who take care of themselves are far better able to be strong and supportive of their children than those parents who do not.*

UNDERSTANDING THE NATURE OF STRESS

In the context of divorce, the word *stress* is best defined as a state of mental or emotional tension that can alter a parent's normal behavior and occurs when he or she is experiencing excessive environmental or psychological pressures.

Even in the friendliest divorces, there is some stress involved. Ending a marriage by definition involves change, and change requires adjustment. We are like thermostats in the way we adjust to change: A thermostat is positioned at a comfortable temperature and turns on or shuts off constantly in order to maintain that perfect temperature.

Likewise, each of us has a comfort zone in which we function best. During a divorce, there are many actions and emotions that can push us out of that comfort zone and into a place of distress, and we must seek out ways to return to our comfortable, higher-functioning spot.

Stress and health are closely linked. Stress contributes to such physical illnesses as high blood pressure, cancer, headaches, and ulcers. Likewise, stress increases a person's potential for emotional ailments like depression, anxiety, insomnia, and panic attacks. The impact of stress on emotional and physical health can be both immediate and long-term. There is also evidence that chronically stressed people tend to seek out alcohol, drugs, or cigarettes and are more likely to have unhealthy eating habits. All of these things directly influence a parent's health in a negative way.

One particularly stressful part of a divorce is the element of the unknown. There are so many concerns that divorcing parents may have that there are no answers for: Are we making the right choice? Will the children be okay? Will we get along better after the divorce? Will I ever fall in love and marry again? Will the children like their new stepparents? Unfortunately, only time can provide the answers to these questions.

The first step in understanding stress is figuring out when you are overwhelmed. In my divorce-parenting classes, I ask the attendees to spend a few moments writing about how they know when they're stressed out. Common responses include biting nails, slamming doors, not sleeping enough or sleeping too much, crying, being short-tempered, showing impatience with the kids, having headaches, feeling unmotivated, experiencing distraction at work, and being unable to complete tasks.

Some actions may be both indicators of stress and the means of relieving it. For instance, smoking or drinking too much may be both a sign of stress and a way in which a parent attempts to take it away. Similarly, many parents describe throwing themselves into their work or cleaning their homes as indicators of stress. Activities such as these are also common skills for coping with stress. Working and cleaning are tasks that bring comfort because they offer the feeling of being in control. A divorcing parent may not have power over the effectiveness of mediation or how his or her ex-spouse treats the children, but the parent can at least be sure that the closets are organized and the spice drawer is alphabetized!

Many parents are simply not conscious of when they are overwhelmed. They often ignore warning signals such as a clenched jaw or irritability. A good example of this comes from a family session I had with a divorcing mom and dad and their four children.

I began the session by commenting on the stress level in the room. One child (a fourteen-year-old boy) said, "Yeah, well if you think this is bad, you should try coming to live at our house for a day or two." A second child (an eleven-year-old girl) added, "You have no idea how bad it gets. This is nothing compared to what it's usually like." The mom piped in, "Oh, c'mon you guys, it's not that bad. . . ." Then, the youngest child (a five-year-old boy) spoke, "When it's really bad, Mom has 'the face.'" The mom looked perplexed and asked, "What are you talking about? What 'face'?" All three children nodded profusely and went on to describe a certain facial expression and body stance Mom had when she was upset. They also described how she walked heavier around the house and pulled open drawers more roughly when she was stressed out. Mom had been unaware of her appearance when she was upset and admitted that after listening to the children, she thought what they said was probably quite accurate.

The second step in understanding stress is identifying what triggers stress for you. In my divorce-parenting classes I ask attendees to jot down what they think is currently causing them stress. Common answers include not enough time to do everything, concern for the kids, meddling in-laws, fighting with the ex-spouse, financial struggles, job pressures, and no help in caring for the children. Sometimes, by listing their triggers, a parent may be able to discover a few situations or people to avoid in order to reduce stress.

When it comes to understanding stress, awareness of being stressed out and what causes your stress is half the battle. The other half is composed of finding ways to relieve it.

CAUSES OF STRESS IN A DIVORCE AND HOW TO MINIMIZE THEM

There are many reasons divorcing parents are at higher risk for stress: the pressures of single parenting, feelings of failure and loss from the marriage ending, financial strains, an increase in fighting, lack of friends or family support, and concerns about the future. The following are some of the contributing factors that can add additional stress to divorcing parents and suggestions for managing these conditions.

Compensating for an Absent Parent

When some parents divorce, they are left to do *everything* alone. Perhaps one parent is incarcerated, is in substance-abuse rehabilitation, or has left the state or country. In these cases, everyday life can be difficult. This is especially true when the remaining parent does not have local family members to help out. Additionally, if the parent does not have prior job training or work experience, he or she may have a hard time financially picking up the slack for the absent parent. In these scenarios, the parent and the children can suffer greatly.

If your ex-spouse has abandoned you, there are a couple of things you can do to help ease your stress.

First, you can ask for help. Asking for help can be one of the most difficult things for some divorcing parents to do. However, getting assistance from family or friends can make a huge difference in your ability to handle stressful situations. Not surprisingly, people are often happy to help a parent who needs it. The following is an example of a client who used a bit of creativity in order to find the help she needed.

One woman ("Margot") in my parenting class came to me during a break and told me, with a great deal of irritation, that asking for help was not an option for her. She went on to explain that her husband was incarcerated and she had no local family support. She was broke and had three children under five years old. She choked up and stated, "There is no time for me."

At her request, I saw Margot for several therapy sessions to help her deal with the lack of support and overwhelming circumstances. I pointed out that therapy was a good start at asking for help so she could do something for herself.

Margot decided to ask a neighbor to watch her children for an hour. Because she had no extra money, she asked the neighbor if they could swap babysitting instead of exchanging cash. This neighbor was a single mom with two young children and was thrilled with the prospect of some time for herself and so she agreed.

Twice a week, for an hour each day, Margot took care of all five children. Two other days during the week, the neighbor reciprocated and Margot had two hours to herself that week. An excellent start indeed! Margot reported spending the time cleaning, grocery shopping, going for a walk, taking a catnap, or just watching some mindless television.

Although Margot thought she had no one to help and it was difficult for her to ask, she reported her arrangement with the neighbor as being one of the best things she ever did.

Some single parents I have seen for therapy have treated themselves to a house cleaner every two weeks to help them out with the many domestic chores that pile up. Other parents have asked friends or family members to help out with picking the kids up from activities. Even sending the kids for an occasional sleepover at a family member's home can help you catch up on some much needed sleep. One single dad I counseled paid his sister to cook a few meals for him and the kids to make life a bit easier during the following week.

Another way of dealing with the reality of having to compensate for an absent parent is to work through the anger. When one parent is absent, the remaining parent may experience a great deal of anger toward the other. Being left alone to parent the children, especially when there are legal or financial issues hanging about, can lead to feelings of resentment. Anger and resentment are emotional drains and take away from the energy you need to expend on everyday parenting tasks. Additionally, these emotions can contribute to more serious ailments like hypertension, depression, or heart attack.

Identifying the root of anger toward a spouse can be helpful. Let's say your spouse has gone to prison for repeated driving-under-the-influence (DUI) arrests and for driving with a suspended license. You then initiate a divorce because it is obvious your spouse has not dealt with his or her substance-abuse issues or is not a functioning member of the family. There are some basic questions you can ask yourself: Am I mad at myself for choosing a spouse I knew had an addiction problem? Am I angry because I have to be the responsible one when my spouse makes these poor choices? Am I angry because of the embarrassment I feel about having my friends and family read about my spouse's arrests in the paper? Am I angry that he or she has chosen alcohol over the marriage? Or am I simply angry at this person for leaving me alone to deal with all this?

The answers to these questions can help you to decide what to focus on in order to work on forgiveness and make clear-cut, less emotional decisions in the future. *Reactive* decisions (those decisions that emanate from feeling angry about what a spouse has said or done) are usually not well thought out and can have negative effects on both you and your children. A far better alternative is to work through the negative feelings (i.e., anger) first before making any serious decisions.

Talking with a neutral friend or family member, a minister, or a therapist can help you work through the feelings that come along with a difficult divorce. Exploring and processing these feelings usually leads to a healthier mind-set and clearer decision-making abilities.

Handling the Financial Strains
Financial stress is perhaps one of the most troublesome burdens a parent can carry during and after divorce. A divorce, especially if it is contested or unfriendly, can end up putting many parents into debt if they were not already in debt prior to the filing. Financial problems are one of the top contributors to marital discord and most certainly one of the top stressors during divorce proceedings.

Consider mediation as a cheaper (and often more amicable) means to divorce. Mediation and collaborative divorce have become increasingly popular alternatives to the traditional divorce route. If this is not possible, a therapist skilled in couples work may be able to help you work through anger and impasses that may arise so that the legal battle is not drawn out any longer than it must be.

During a divorce, many parents benefit from creating a new budget for themselves that reflects the changes that may have occurred in their family. Perhaps there are new legal bills, an additional rental payment for the parent who may have moved out, or less cash flow due to frozen assets. The vast majority of parents who go through a divorce find they must tighten their belts, at least initially.

Don't be afraid to ask for help. Many clients have told me that a simple explanatory call to service providers like the electric company often results in an extended grace period or a temporary rate reduction. Family members may be able to help out as well with free child care or picking up some extra groceries or meals.

Dealing with an Increase in Fighting

Some divorcing parents report a reduction in fighting after one parent moves out, but for many others, the fighting escalates regardless of the living arrangements. An increase in fighting is not only detrimental for the children to witness, but it can also be draining on the parents who participate in the continual bickering.

Some parents are successful in sitting down with each other and setting clear boundaries for how they will avoid confrontation. If this option fails, you may want to consider communicating *only* via handwritten notes, voice mail, or e-mail. A note of caution, though—these types of communication can be retained by one parent and used in court against the other parent. As with *any* communication, *utilize extreme care in anything you say, write, or type.*

Couples therapy may be beneficial in helping you communicate in a healthier manner when there is an increase in fighting. It's a common myth that marriage counseling is solely meant for saving marriages. For many couples, especially those who seek treatment prior to knowing whether they will stay married, therapy can greatly improve communication. Couples work can help divorce proceedings go more smoothly too.

Another helpful hint is to talk to someone other than your spouse about your frustrations and concerns. Sometimes this venting can alleviate some of the stress, thereby reducing the level of anger in subsequent conversations with your spouse. If you are able to talk to someone else about these stresses, you will be able to get feedback *prior* to speaking with your spouse. Like a trial run, this allows the third party or the therapist to point out things you should avoid saying, in order to reduce the intensity of the discussion with your spouse.

Lacking the Support of Family and Friends

A divorce can be particularly traumatic for a parent who does not have the support of friends or family. Sometimes this occurs when members of the parent's support system live out of state or are deceased. Other times, family members and friends may take the side of the other parent, thereby leaving one parent feeling unsupported. In any case, feeling alone during a divorce can be a huge stressor on a parent.

Going through a divorce is not regularly the topic of discussion around watercoolers at work or pickup lines at preschool. For this reason, many parents fail to recognize just how *not* alone they are when going through a divorce. Over 4.8 million Americans go through this process each year. Although the individual details of each divorce vary greatly, all parents who divorce share many of the same feelings and experiences.

If you feel you need support, don't be afraid to call up neighbors or coworkers who you know are divorced. Having been through it themselves, they may be able to offer support or provide suggestions. Look into single-parent or divorce support groups in lieu of having friends and family around. Seeking out an individual therapist for assistance during the divorce is yet another option. There are many other resources (such as books and websites; see Appendix A) available that may help bolster you when other supports are simply not around. One of my personal favorites is divorcemagazine.com, which contains cutting-edge information on a variety of topics as well as an active online forum to ask questions or share experiences.

Worrying About the Future

One of the scariest things divorcing parents may feel is worry about the future. Of course parents are concerned about how their children will adjust to the divorce, but many parents worry about how *they* will fare after the divorce as well.

No parent has a crystal ball that allows him or her to look into the future. Nor are there easy answers to the questions parents want to ask: Will I ever feel less angry? Will I ever come to terms with this decision? Will I be able to make it financially on my own?

Remember that divorce is a *process*. Feelings transform over time, and adjustment to family changes eventually happens. You will most likely *not* feel the same way you do now in a few months or a few years. Your sense of worry will probably decrease a bit as each stage of the divorce process takes place. Take comfort in knowing that many parents eventually do find contentment and a good quality of life after divorce.

In the interim, when feelings of concern are high, try to focus on self-care. Journaling, praying, talking to friends, exercising, and good nutrition can help offset the negative effects of worry. Focusing on the positive can be an effective tool for parents as well. You may also find great consolation in remembering the reasons you chose to divorce and how the divorce will improve the future of the entire family.

And remember that regardless of what the future holds for you, you will still have the most wonderful gift in your life—*your children*. Channel your feelings of worry into making the here-and-now experiences with your children the best they can be.

Continuing to Live with an Ex-Spouse
When I first started teaching divorce-parenting classes many years ago, most parents who had filed for divorce were living separately; when the couple decided to split, one parent moved out. Today, however, some parents may agree to remain living in the same home for a period of time.

There are a couple of reasons why this situation is becoming increasingly common. First and foremost is the cost of living. Many former couples find it simply impossible to afford separate residences. When parents are scrambling to come up with a great deal of money for mediators and/or lawyers, there is often not much cash left over for anything else.

Another explanation for this rise in living together during divorce proceedings is the housing market in general. If a couple owns a home together and has been unable to sell it, the couple may not be able to extract enough money for separate housing.

I recently bumped into a couple I had in my divorce-parenting class almost a year and a half earlier. These parents said they had a very large home together and could not sell it; the bad housing market left them stuck living together nearly nine months after their divorce was final. This situation proved to be very stressful for both parents, as they had both begun dating other people. It was awkward to share space with an ex-spouse and share a totally different life with another romantic partner. In addition, because the children were in the home, the parents felt uncomfortable staying out overnight or even coming home late. This arrangement took a huge toll on each of their new relationships.

If you are a parent who must live with your ex-partner in the same residence, there are several things you can do to minimize the inherent stress in this situation. For instance, consider trying to create a schedule with your spouse that decreases the amount of time you are actually in the home with each other. This is especially important if you and your ex-spouse are prone to arguing. Perhaps Dad could plan on going to the gym on nights when Mom is home, and Dad could be home on the nights Mom has her book club meeting and yoga class. This arrangement also ensures that children have quality time with both Mom and Dad and helps them get used to how things will be when Mom and Dad no longer live in the same home.

One parent can also consider moving out of the marital bedroom. If it is possible, each individual should have a separate sleeping area. Having this space allows each of you to have a "safe haven" or a place to be alone. Ideally, this spot would have a television or computer desk so that either of you can use the area to do work and have some downtime as well. This setup can lessen the annoyance or anxiety each may feel toward the other, and it can reduce conflict. All of these things can positively affect the children's experience while you both remain in the same home.

Finally, when divorcing couples must live together, it is important that each parent have an opportunity to experience living alone (without the other parent). One way to ease into this is for both you and your ex-spouse to have a night out. On this night, if either of you wishes, the other can crash at a friend's house or spend the night at a hotel or with relatives. This allows an escape for the parent who may have to live in a setting that may be uncomfortable the rest of the time. It also affords the opportunity to date or just stay out late without the children being directly aware of it. This night out helps children get used to one parent at a time doing the parenting. Additionally, everyone will begin to have a feel for what the household will be like when one parent is not there.

Dealing with Mental Health or Substance-Abuse Issues

Some parents will experience stress over leaving their children with their ex-spouses if there is a serious mental health or substance-abuse issue. This stress can be compounded if the spouse denies there is a problem and the parent is stuck in a he-said/she-said battle. Documentation and legal intervention take time in these situations. In the meantime, the parent may be required to allow the children to visit alone with the mentally ill or substance-abusing spouse.

Obviously, a parent in this situation will experience a great deal of concern over the children's safety and well-being. This is perhaps one of the worst feelings any parent can suffer during a divorce. In fact, some parents will stay in a deteriorating marriage just to avoid having to leave the children alone with an ill spouse.

Perhaps the most important thing you can do in this situation is to channel your fears and negative energies appropriately. Working with a lawyer, a family service agency, or the court to address such serious concerns should be the first course of action.

In the interim, you may also want to discuss boundaries and coping skills with your children to help prepare them for time spent with a parent who suffers from serious mental health issues or addiction. For instance, parents can instruct a child to call a trusted family member if he or she feels uncomfortable with a parent's behavior or witnesses a parent drinking too much. You can also tuck a list of contact numbers and a cell phone in the child's overnight bag. And the child could use a special code word to signify discomfort when the other parent calls to check in.

Perhaps the saddest part of having a child who spends time with a parent with a mental health or substance-abuse issue is explaining these illnesses to the child. Mental illness and addiction are often difficult to talk about with children. Most parents wish they did not have to clutter their young children's heads with these serious topics prematurely. However, if children are experiencing a parent's maltreatment, bizarre behavior, extreme emotions, or drug or alcohol use, it is important to discuss these things with them immediately.

One problem is that parents often end up criticizing their ex-spouses to some degree during the explanation process. It is vital that you and your ex-spouse strive to talk about these issues in a calm and informative manner that is as devoid of judgment as possible. Certainly, you can make clear that you do not support the other parent's choice to use substances or that certain behaviors are simply unacceptable.

The bottom line is that a parent's discussion with a child about these matters should serve two main purposes. The first purpose is to give the child some understanding of what he or she is experiencing. This is so that the child will not misconstrue the occurrences as somehow being the child's fault. Additionally, the child should acquire some knowledge about the issue and what drives the parent to act the way he or she does sometimes.

The second purpose is to help the child understand his or her rights to healthy care and treatment from the parent. If the child is uncomfortable or feels he or she is in danger, he or she should be empowered to know what to do to feel safe.

Having Concerns About an Ex-Spouse's New Significant Other

During some divorces, one parent may have great concerns about his or her children spending time with the other parent's new partner. This is particularly the case when a parent moves in with a new romantic interest and that boyfriend or girlfriend is frequently present during the parenting time.

It is often hard to get to know your ex-spouse's new partner. As would be expected, not knowing anything about someone may leave you hesitant to have your children be around this "stranger."

One way to help ease your or your ex-spouse's anxiety about a new relationship is providing the opportunity to talk to the new boyfriend or girlfriend. If all parties agree and can be civil to each other, arrange a meeting to discuss concerns or thoughts on parenting. Hearing Dad's new girlfriend say, "I have no interest in replacing the children's mother and feel strongly that I should hang back and let Dad do the parenting at this point," can be hugely comforting for a concerned mom to hear.

Sometimes, however, this scenario is not an option. Feelings of jealousy or anger can prevent one of you from being in the presence of the other parent's new significant other. This is especially true when a spouse has had an affair with this person during the course of the marriage. If this is the case, one of you may consider writing down some concerns or questions and giving them to the other parent and his or her new partner for perusal. They may then read the issues listed and respond in writing. In this manner, some written communication may help one parent to feel more comfortable with the ex-spouse's new partner and his or her involvement with the children.

Some parents I have counseled have found some success in giving the children a "warming up" period when introducing them to a parent's new boyfriend or girlfriend. For example, the parents may concur that for the first six months of the relationship, the time each parent spends with the children will be without the new significant other. This conversation and "contract" is ideal, however, and for some parents there simply won't be any agreement.

Sometimes, it is the children themselves who are uncomfortable with their parents' new partners. This is the story of one family I saw for therapy regarding this issue.

"Brett" and "Shelby" had two children together, "Christopher" and "Chelsea." They had recently filed for divorce because Shelby learned that Brett had been having an affair with a coworker, "Liz." Brett immediately moved into Liz's home. Shelby demanded that Brett spend his parenting time without Liz and outside of her home. Shelby argued that it was both immoral and too confusing for the kids to see their father living with another woman before the divorce was final. She also expressed great concern about not knowing anything about Liz and not having any reason to trust her being around Christopher and Chelsea.

Brett initially agreed with Shelby's wishes and took his children to his sister's house to spend every other weekend with them. On his weeknight with the children, Brett would take them out for dinner or to a movie or a mall.

Soon, Brett grew weary of the arrangement. He was frequently fighting with his sister as she began criticizing his children and his parenting style. Brett was also running out of things to do with the kids on his weeknight and he found he was spending far too much money on fast food and entertainment. By this time, Brett had been living with Liz for nearly five months and felt that Christopher and Chelsea should be able to spend time with him where he was living. The children already knew that he was in a serious relationship with Liz and that he lived with her. Brett argued that it was silly at this point to send him schlepping around town with Christopher and Chelsea when he should just be able to have them with him at his home.

Shelby stood her ground on her view that the children should not be exposed to the seriousness of Brett's relationship with Liz until after the divorce was complete. Her attorney fought long and hard to keep the arrangement in place. However, after several delays with the divorce proceedings and some fierce insistence from Brett's lawyer that the children be allowed to spend time with Dad at Liz's house, both parties compromised.

The ultimate agreement was as follows: The family was required to engage in therapy with me. I was expected to hold at least two sessions with Brett and Liz in order to assess whether they had appropriate parenting skills and especially whether Liz understood her boundary with the children in terms of overstepping Brett's parenting role. The children would first be introduced to Liz through a series of five outside visits with Brett (out to eat, bowling, etc.). If the children did not protest seeing Brett at his home at this point, they would then be allowed to stay with him on his "every other weekend," but Liz would not sleep in the same bedroom as Brett during these overnights until after the divorce was finalized.

In the end, Brett and Liz "passed" their sessions with flying colors and this allowed Shelby to become a bit more comfortable with Liz's involvement in her children's lives. The slow integration of Liz and Brett's new residence into the children's lives seemed to work well for everyone. Of course, Brett and Liz did not have to agree to this arrangement, but in doing so they gently helped both Shelby and the children get used to the new situation.

Possibly the best reason you and your former partner should consider limiting the time the children initially spend with a new significant other is simple: You just cannot be sure in the beginning whether a new relationship will last very long. During a time of significant loss for children, it is not wise to subject the children to other unnecessary losses. As a rule of thumb, it's best to try to limit your children's exposure to a new partner until the relationship is fairly promising and serious.

RELIEVING STRESS

When parents become more able to recognize signs of stress and things that trigger it, the next step is doing something to alleviate it. Doing so allows children to have more positive interactions with their parents and experience less stress themselves. Parents who actively manage their stress set an excellent example for their children as well. The following suggestions are ways that divorcing parents can reduce stress and prioritize their own well-being.

Take a Parenting Class Early On
Although not all are mandatory, parenting classes for divorcing moms and dads are available in almost every state. These classes can offer you

and your ex-spouse a great deal of information you may not otherwise receive. Having this insight can help you both to avoid some of the worst stress-inducing pitfalls for yourselves and for your children.

Too often, parents take my class a few days before their final court dates. Unfortunately, by the time they reach my class, these parents may have already made several errors that most negatively affect their children. Taking the class at the very beginning of the divorce process ensures that you will know how to decrease the trauma your children may experience.

Sometimes I have parents who begrudgingly attend the divorce-parenting class. I remind them that the class will probably be the only time they will ever have six full, uninterrupted hours to focus on their children's well-being and best interests.

In addition to parenting classes and the many books available on divorce-parenting issues, we are also fortunate to have the Internet. There are innumerable websites for divorcing parents that offer valuable information and advice on a variety of topics. A few good sites to begin with are www.divorcesource.com, www.divorcesupport.com, and www.divorcenet.com. Even Dr. Phil's website (www.drphil.com) frequently contains good advice, discussions, and links for divorcing parents. Doing a search for "matrimonial lawyers" in your state will also turn up more local information sites.

Take Care of Personal Issues

Divorce is one of the most stressful experiences in life. If you are a parent who has a history of drinking too much or having bouts of depression when life becomes overwhelming, now is the time to get help for these issues. In order to remain focused on the very important parenting issues during divorce, you need to be as emotionally strong and healthy as possible.

A treatment program, therapy, or even Alcoholics Anonymous meetings can lend support if either you or your ex-spouse is struggling with the pain of divorce, especially if it is a less-than-amicable split. This support can give you much-needed time for venting and better coping skills to deal with the stress.

Consider asking family members or friends to help out with the kids if you have had too much to drink or are battling depression. Children can become burdened with worry for a parent if they see that parent drunk, passed out, or unable to get out of bed for days on end. It is of utmost importance that if either of you is predisposed to these types of responses, you get the help you need . . . *for the children's sake.*

Don't Always Listen to Others

Talking to a good friend or family member can be tremendously helpful in reducing stress for a divorcing parent. Conversely, though, certain friends or family members can make the situation more stressful.

It can be difficult for a friend or family member who loves and cares about a parent to remain neutral. This person may unknowingly come off as critical when he or she tells the parent, "You deserve so much better," or "Why do you even give that jerk the time of day?" This person may also feel invested in what he or she thinks the divorcing parent needs to do to feel better. For example, one divorcing dad I saw had a good friend who kept fixing him up with blind dates or getting single women at work to call him up and ask him out. This friend thought the attention would make the dad feel good about himself and help him realize all the women who were out there waiting for him. However, the dad expressed to me that he just wasn't ready to get back into dating and simply had no interest in these women. In fact, he said the phone calls made things worse in that they reminded him he was no longer married.

Be careful in choosing whom you confide in. Seek out friends and family members who are good listeners, supportive, and honest. It is okay to tell someone graciously that he or she is not being helpful to you or is making you feel pressured or uncomfortable. Sometimes friends and family members forget that they cannot do this for you; the divorce and healing process is different for every parent and one he or she ultimately must figure out alone.

Make Time for Yourself

Making time for yourself is perhaps the most essential thing you can do to relieve stress during a divorce. Things can often feel overwhelming during this time. Personal time to relax, catch up, or refocus can be enormously beneficial for your physical or emotional state. Additionally, doing something you enjoy can remind you that happiness and life in general do go on after a divorce.

Many parents complain they do not have the time to do something for themselves after working and caring for the children and the home. But even the simplest of things can make a difference. For example, carving out a ten-minute personal transition time between coming home from work and jumping into the dinner–homework–bath routine can be a destressing measure parents can take. Use those precious moments to unwind with the newspaper, flip through the TV channels, or just relax and gear up for the next wave of chaos in the home. You might be surprised how much momentum those few minutes can give you.

"Margot," my client who, as you may recall, swapped babysitting with a neighbor, is also a good example of finding time for oneself even when there is no time.

With her husband incarcerated, no local family support, and three preschool-age children, Margot found herself burning the proverbial candle at both ends. In my sessions with Margot, we discussed the need for her to find "me time," as she was growing increasingly more irritable and tired. She agreed but remained adamant that there was just not enough time in the day for her to do something for herself.

After several brainstorming sessions, Margot came in one week quite excited about an idea she had come up with for finding "me time." She explained that she had invited her three little ones to bring several dolls and stuffed animals into the bathroom. There she set up a plastic tea set with real juice inside and a plate of animal crackers. The children could have the tea party there while Margot soaked in a hot tub she had drawn for herself, complete with bubbles and candles aglow. Margot could then monitor the children, but because they were in a contained area, she could also rest a bit and enjoy an indulgent bath. The children were thrilled to dress up their dolls and animals for the party and to pour real juice into the teacups. Margot was equally thrilled that the bathroom floor was vinyl and juice spills were easy to wipe up.

This setup became a twice-a-week ritual for Margot and her children, and in fact, the children begged for this opportunity nearly every day. Even when it appeared there was no possible way for Margot to indulge in something for herself, she was able to find a little something that made a huge difference in her everyday routine.

Especially during the trying times of a divorce and the strains of single parenting, you and your former spouse need to take care of yourselves. There are a number of simple things you can do that can help reduce some of the stress you may be experiencing.

For example, getting enough sleep is a vital part of any person's functioning. Many parents who are going through a divorce report not sleeping well. Don't view sleep as an indulgence; it is a necessity for good emotional and physical health.

If you know you are not getting enough sleep, consider letting something else slide in order to go to bed earlier. Try hitting the sack when the kids do one night, even if that means at 7:30 p.m. sharp. Or arrange to take a nap. There is a great deal of research in support of the health benefits of a short nap during the day. You might consider sitting down with your children and asking what it would take for them to give you an hour of quiet, uninterrupted time for a nap. If they promise to let you sleep for an hour and they make good on their promise, perhaps you can then agree to play a board game or take them out for ice cream afterward. This fosters a sense of unity and working together as a family.

Many divorcing parents who take my class cite prayer as a helpful destressing tool. Prayer is not only for deeply religious people. In fact, a basic sense of spirituality can help you put your concerns into the hands of a higher power. Praying allows you to sort of talk through what you may be feeling and offer these thoughts up to the ultimate in neutral parties. Praying to a higher power permits you to express things and ask for help without being criticized, pressured, or given unwanted feedback.

Laughter can be a very potent medicine as well. There is a great deal of research on the health benefits of laughing. Plan to go out with a funny friend or rent a comedy to watch one night. Observe the silliness in children's play. Finding lightness in a time of sadness and darkness can be very helpful.

Exercise can be beneficial in many ways. Working out can improve your overall health, help you lose unhealthy extra pounds, and release hormones that can help you to have more energy and feel better. Exercising sends a healthful message to your children as well and can be an excellent way for a family to connect and spend time together.

Exercise need not be an hour at the gym each day, but rather any physical effort. Going bowling or hiking with the kids are great ways to get some exercise. Meditation or yoga can be done almost anywhere, and you can remain in the home and watching over your children, if need be, while engaging in it. Sledding and walking the dog are other great ways to get out and get active.

Small indulgences can help stressful times seem a bit lighter, too, even if only temporarily. Lounging in bed one day until noon while reading a romance novel is not a sin, nor is stopping into a chocolate shop for a decadent truffle while shopping at the mall. Some parents report ordering in Chinese food on occasion when they are really too tired to cook. Others swear by a glass of wine and a cheesy movie.

These indulgences are especially effective when they are spur of the moment, particularly when they are in place of something you know you should be doing, such as cleaning the bathroom. Giving in to yourself once in a while can help you remember that life is full of small pleasures.

Physical contact can be a bolstering factor against stress for parents going through a divorce. For many parents, positive physical contact between them dwindled away long ago. Hugs and snuggles from your children can be wonderful but sometimes may not be enough. Consider hanging out with a physically demonstrative friend or getting a professional massage. There is even research that suggests petting a dog or cuddling a furry pet can have healthful benefits like lowering the heart rate. The power of touch can be very effective in making you feel better.

Many parents going through a divorce do not feel good about themselves, especially physically. Perhaps a parent is carrying a little extra "baby weight" or his or her spouse had an affair, so the parent may not feel he or she was attractive enough to the ex-spouse. In any case, feeling attractive and good about oneself can be powerful tools.

If you are feeling a little down on yourself, consider doing something about it. Start walking in the morning before work or buy a treadmill to lose some extra pounds. Consider a new haircut or a manicure. Buy yourself a new outfit. Sometimes it may simply be getting up a few minutes earlier to get ready for work. This can give you that extra little effort that makes you feel better about your appearance.

Sometimes, an overwhelmed parent must learn to say no to certain things in order to retain his or her sanity. During a stressful time like divorce, you and your former partner should consider turning down invitations to parties you really don't want to attend or passing on the sign-up list for volunteers for a work-related task force. Saying no to frivolous things leaves you both more time and energy for the more important things you must accomplish.

Many divorcing parents I counsel report that fantasizing is a good destressing technique. Fantasizing about a different life, writing the next best-selling novel, or locking eyes with an incredibly attractive stranger can provide you with a momentary lapse of reality. These escapes can have powerful positive effects.

I frequently use individualized relaxation and imagery techniques with stressed clients I see for therapy. I have them practice picturing their perfect spot. Perhaps it is a Caribbean beach. I will then help them imagine all the details—feeling the hot sand between their toes, and hearing the seagulls circling above, the gentle lapping of low-tide ocean waves, and distant sounds of children's laughter. With practice, many clients can find this place in their minds and use it as an escape during stressful moments.

During sad and dark times like divorce, it can be difficult for parents to remember the beauty all around them. Some parents have told me that just stopping whatever they were doing and sitting down to play with their children reminded them of what was really important in life. Yet others have described how looking at nature or planting brightly colored flowers in their yard brought simple beauty to their lives.

If you are a parent caught up in the negative forces of divorce, take a moment to find something beautiful around you. Witnessing a tender moment between two strangers on the street can help you remember how wonderful love is and that it exists.

Your mind-set is perhaps the most influential device you have for dealing with stress. The mind has the ability to reason and help you make sense of what's going on. Remember the old adage "mind over matter"?

Many divorcing parents I have counseled have told me how their constructive mind-sets have helped them get through difficult times. One dad whom I saw for therapy described how he took one particularly overwhelming day and forced himself to think through each of the stressors that were plaguing him, piece by piece. When he was done, he had adjusted his mind-set, understood that he could not do everything, and knew it would be better to narrow it all down to a few priorities he needed to follow through on. He expressed feeling some relief with this view and also empowerment to make changes in a few areas he knew were important. Likewise, talking with a trusted friend, family member, or therapist about your difficulties can help you understand the stressors in a different light.

One of the most common mind-set techniques is to look at the proverbial glass as half full rather than as half empty. It is easy to get caught up in all that is crappy right now without acknowledging all that is good in life as well.

As a therapist, I see how many people suffer in life each day. This allows me to see how "half full" my own life is. One divorcing mom I saw for therapy described her own way of turning a half-empty day into a half-full one.

> My family thinks I'm nuts for doing this, but it's the only thing that seems to work when I'm having one of those "poor me" days. I force myself to sit down at the computer and look up sites for horrid conditions in Russian orphanages, poverty in war-torn African towns, and unspeakable cases of animal abuse. After perusing these sites for a while, you'd think I'd be more depressed. But no, I actually feel a sense of relief and almost joy. I'm able to realize all the sadness around me and see how lucky I am for all that I have. Healthy children who are safe. We never have to worry about a roof over our heads and food on our table. This is how I put the rotten stuff in my own life into a healthier perspective.

Finally, some parents deal with stress by giving themselves daily positive reminders of what's important in life. I have asked some parents to write down on little Post-it Notes two of their most redeeming strengths or qualities. I have them stick these little reminders in common areas, like on the bathroom mirror or the refrigerator door, so they will see them several times a day.

One divorcing parent I saw for therapy cut out a couple of her most affirming statements from magazines, laminated them, glued little pieces of magnet on the back, and put them around her home and office to keep her thinking in a positive way. She described her encounters with these words of wisdom as being very supportive to her during one of the saddest times of her life.

*   *   *

If you and your ex-spouse can remember that taking care of yourselves is related directly to taking better care of your children, you will be investing time wisely when you carve out "me time." If you take good care of yourselves, you will both be better equipped to withstand the stresses of divorce and single parenting.

4

Managing Parenting
Time with Your
Children and
Ex-Spouse

Quality parenting time with children is one of the most important things for parents to focus on during and after divorce. However, working out the details of single-parenting tasks and transitions between two homes and environments can sometimes be challenging. This chapter addresses the ins and outs of parenting time and offers practical suggestions to help manage the intricacies of this vital time for parent and child.

TRENDS IN DIVORCE INVOLVING CHILDREN

In recent years, a few important changes have improved today's divorce experience compared with divorces of the past. Among the most significant modifications frequently found in modern-day divorces are a new language, a new mind-set, the increased involvement of fathers in parenting, shared parenting, and more regular involvement with the children.

A New Language and a New Mind-Set
One of the simplest changes to divorce "lingo" is that the word *visitation* has been replaced with the term *parenting time*. This reflects a

wonderful change in mind-set: *Parents who divorce should be engaged with their children as parents rather than interacting with them as visitors.* The regular, healthy involvement of both parents in a child's life after divorce is an important part of the child's well-being.

In previous decades, many parents felt slighted and offended by the new role of "visiting parent" that was given to them after the divorce. These parents felt the acute loss of being demoted from "parent" to "visitor." Although it's simply a subtle shift of words, this change to *parenting time* has given divorcing parents the right to retain the role of "parent" in whatever postdivorce capacity they wish.

The children benefit as well; they are free to engage fully with *both* parents rather than forced to reduce one parent to the limited role of "visiting parent."

The Increased Involvement of Fathers in Parenting

Another important change in recent years is that fathers in particular have taken a much bigger role in parenting than they did in past decades. Courts have recognized this development and now consider fathers and mothers more equally when the preferred joint custody arrangement is not possible for safety reasons. In fact, the number of fathers seeking (and winning) sole custody is far greater than ever before.

Shared Parenting

In addition, a growing number of divorced parents share everyday parenting tasks more equally. Not only do more parents share physical custody more evenly between their homes, but they often split routine child-rearing issues 50-50 as well. For example, more divorcing parents are opting for alternating who takes the children to their pediatric appointments, who goes on class field trips, and even who will host a child's sleepover.

More Regular Involvement with the Children

Finally, the popularity of and accessibility to better technology allows divorced parents to remain more involved with their children when they are with the other parent. Cell phones, e-mail, instant messaging, Skype, and FaceTime permit a parent to be in contact with a child on a more regular basis. Such technological improvements have allowed divorced parents to maintain a constant relationship with their children even if they now live far away. This frequent contact can help soften the blow of having one parent move out of the town or state postdivorce.

The aforementioned trends have all had a positive impact on families going through divorce. These changes have also made it easier for children to experience the presence of *both* parents in their lives after the divorce is final.

PROBLEMS WITH PARENTING TIME

Given the importance of quality parenting time for children of divorce, it is equally important to address some of the struggles and pitfalls that can occur during this special time between parent and child. The following is a discussion of some of the most common issues that can interfere with healthy parenting time and suggestions for how to help make things go more smoothly.

The Individualized Needs of the Children

No parenting plan exists that can account for all the unexpected situations that will inevitably occur in raising children. Parenting plans rarely take into account the individualized needs of any one specific child. For instance, the plan may clearly delineate that one parent will spend Wednesday evenings and every other weekend with the children, but it may omit certain particular circumstances.

For instance, should the parent who has the children on Wednesday evenings ever have responsibilities for orthodontic appointments, soccer practice, or school play rehearsals that occur on other days of the week? What if a child gets sick several times during the school year and it never once happens on a Wednesday? Should the "Wednesday parent" take time off on some of these sick days to be home with the child? What if one child suffers from a serious learning disability and attends a specialized school that has a parent meeting the last Friday of every month? Should the Wednesday parent be required to attend this meeting once in a while? And what if one child is happy with the Wednesday/every other Friday arrangement but his or her sibling is intolerably missing the parent and asking for more time with that parent?

One set of parents I saw for therapy worked out a parenting arrangement that served the special needs of one of their children.

"Katie" and "Colin" had three daughters: "Brianna" (age seven), "Isabella" (age eleven), and "Kylie" (age fourteen). Katie and Colin had recently separated and filed for divorce. Both reported feeling that single parenting was overwhelming. One particular problem they encountered was that their middle daughter, Isabella, had learning disabilities and some emotional issues. Isabella needed much more assistance and direction with completing homework and other simple tasks than Brianna and Kylie did. Katie and Colin both struggled with being able to give Isabella the attention she required and recently they reported she had begun to have more frequent angry outbursts and meltdowns.

First, I made a referral for Isabella to see an individual therapist to give her support and coping skills during this difficult time. Then, I worked with Katie and Colin to see how they could help each other meet Isabella's special needs. They worked out an arrangement where each compromised a bit on the parenting plan. Colin volunteered to stop by Katie's house two nights a week to help Isabella with schoolwork and getting packed up for school the next day. The two also ended these nights with one of Isabella's favorite card games.

While Colin was giving undivided attention to Isabella, Katie would enjoy some time with Brianna and Kylie. In return, on Colin's every other weekend with the girls, Katie would retain Isabella for a few hours on those Saturday mornings while Colin spent some time with Brianna and Kylie. Sometimes Katie would take Isabella out for breakfast, and other times she would help her catch up on cleaning her room or with schoolwork she might be struggling with. By noon, they'd all meet up and Colin would take the girls for the rest of the weekend.

Colin and Katie noticed an improvement in Isabella's behavior right away and the entire family benefited from splitting up the special time spent with each parent.

Special circumstances may warrant some tweaking of the basic parenting plan both parents agreed to in court. *The ideal way for parents to deal with the unique needs of any one child is through frequent communication and flexibility.* Unfortunately, this is very difficult to do for many divorcing parents. There are some parents who simply do not care to be involved in the everyday workings of a child's life. Yet others have jobs that do not allow for unexpected time off. However, if you both are truly invested in what's best for your children, you will at least try to work together on special issues regarding your children's needs.

Equal Parenting Time When One Parent Is Less Involved

A common complaint I hear from parents is that their divorce gave one parent an equal share in parenting when he or she had very little involvement with the children during the marriage. As you might expect, a parent may feel resentful about this. But there is good news—many parents, even if they had little involvement with their children during the marriage, really step up to the plate and take their new parenting roles more seriously after a divorce. Try to remain hopeful that your ex-spouse will be one of these parents who begins a special new relationship with his or her children once the divorce is final.

Failure to Follow the Parenting Plan

Many divorcing parents I meet complain that the other parent has the right to parent half the time but then does not do much of the parenting after all. As a general rule, *all* divorcing parents should strive to stick to the parenting plan and to contribute what each said he or she would. However, in many cases this does not happen.

Keep in mind that you are not in control of the extent to which the other parent wishes to be involved in the parenting of a child. As frustrating as it can be, if the other parent consistently does not follow through on parenting plan arrangements, there may not be a great deal you can do about it. Hiring an attorney to change the plan or the child support payments to reflect the other parent's lack of involvement is an option, albeit an expensive one for many parents. Otherwise, just try to bear with the circumstances and have back-up plans for times when your former husband or wife doesn't come through.

Not all deviations from the parenting plan are malicious. Sometimes, a parent truly wants half-time parenting but is overestimating his or her ability to follow through. Take the following example of a former client and her two young sons.

"Patrice" was a thirty-seven-year-old divorced mother of two boys: "Calvin" (age six) and "Andy" (age eight). The parenting plan she and her ex-husband, "Paul," drew up provided that Paul would pick up Calvin and Andy every Friday night after work and keep them until Saturday night. Initially, this arrangement was agreeable to both parents. But then, after almost seven months of Paul being inconsistent with his Friday-night pickups, Patrice was beginning to feel frustrated and angry.

Paul had a job in a big city and often got delayed in heavy traffic coming home. He was frequently late and had to cancel altogether on a few occasions. On those few nights that traffic was especially bad, Paul said he wouldn't be able to get there until after the boys' bedtime and he'd just plan on picking them up first thing in the morning. Consequently, Patrice would have to cancel her plans to have dinner with friends and instead would have to deal with Calvin and Andy's frustration and disappointment.

Every Friday night Calvin and Andy knelt on the couch and stared out the living room window patiently awaiting their father's arrival. Because Paul was rarely on time, Patrice would say things like, "Come on away from the window, boys. You might be waiting a very long time. You know Daddy is usually late, so why bother watching? I don't want you to waste your time and be disappointed."

Patrice reported that Calvin and Andy were beginning to get nasty with her when she said these things to them. They would get defensive and shout, "You don't know anything, Mom! He will too be here soon!" Patrice was concerned about their levels of anger.

When I asked Patrice, "Will the boys be disappointed if Paul is late or calls to cancel?" she replied, "Of course." Then I asked, "Will the boys still be disappointed if Paul doesn't show even if you warn them of that possibility?" Patrice thought about the question for a moment and then nodded her head yes. We decided that there were no words to prevent Calvin and Andy the pain and disappointment if Paul was late or didn't show.

So from then on, rather than warning Calvin and Andy about the possibility of disappointment, Patrice changed her method to distraction. She would plan to bake cookies, play a board game, or rent a movie the boys really loved during the time before she expected Paul to arrive. If there was a delay in Paul's pickup time, Calvin and Andy already would be engaged in something fun, which helped soften the blow of his absence. This arrangement worked out better for everyone in the family.

The "Playland Parent"

Back in the day when fathers were mostly the "visiting" parents, the term *Disneyland Dad* was coined. This term described the father who would visit his children and take them somewhere fun, such as Disneyland, for the day. He would then return them home to the mother in an overstimulated state with tummy aches from too much junk food. She was left to deal with the moaning, "bouncing off walls," and constant pleading to do something fun instead of chores and homework. In other words: Daddy = fun, Mommy = no fun.

For this book, I changed *Disneyland Dad* to *Playland Parent* to reflect the recent change in fathers' roles. The Playland Parent still exists in many forms and can be either the father *or* the mother. When I write about this phenomenon, I do not mean an occasional fun-packed outing. The Playland Parent is the one who does *all* the fun stuff, *all* the time. He or she is the one who spends money on whatever the kids want to buy, takes them bowling and to the movies every weekend, and feeds them fast food and takeout without considering whether they are eating healthy or well-rounded meals. This is *not* the parent who deals with homework, hygiene, doctor's appointments, making the bed, feeding the hamster, friendship crises, or boo-boos.

When this situation occurs, it can cause a great deal of stress for both the children and the non–Playland Parent. The children will often have a difficult time adjusting to the return home after such adventurous days. Many times, resentment or competition builds between the parents. The result is that the children expect a good time from the Playland Parent and complain to and resist the other parent.

There are several reasons a parent may choose to be the Playland Parent. Some Playland Parents assume the other parent is doing all the "important" stuff like making sure everyone is doing homework and eating vegetables, so he or she does not think it's a big deal to be the one to let the kids eat junk and have fun. Other Playland Parents tend to overindulge their children due to feelings of guilt about the divorce. And yet other Playland Parents do it specifically to hurt and undermine the other parent.

Regardless of the reason one parent takes on the fun-parent role, there are a couple of approaches you can try to combat the damage this setup can cause. First, when it's the Playland Parent's parenting time, you can send along a list of a few things for the parent to do with your child.

A good rule of thumb is always to *start small*. For example, give the other parent a little note *kindly* asking if he or she could help the child out with some tasks. Perhaps you can ask the parent to pick out a birthday gift and card for the child's playmate who is having a party the following day (always have a back-up gift to give in case the parent forgets or refuses). Or you can ask the other parent if he or she has time to quiz the child on multiplication facts, help the child research a topic online for a science-fair project idea, pick up supplies for a geography assignment due next week, or pick up some shin guards for the child's new soccer season.

You can also consider getting someone else to request the Playland Parent's involvement in the child's life. For instance, if the school calls regarding a behavioral issue, you can have the school call the other parent as well and arrange for him or her to be present for a parent-teacher conference regarding this problem. Likewise, a dentist's office might be willing to call the other parent to discuss a payment issue or schedule the next cleaning appointment. Sometimes the Playland Parent will respond more positively to an outside request for involvement than to a request from the other parent.

Most parents, whether Playland Parents or not, are generally more receptive to assisting the *children* with tasks and chores than they are with helping the *other parents* with these things. When the Playland Parent has experienced the initial reward of helping the child with an important task, he or she may often be more willing to do so again in the future.

If the Playland Parent's motive is to hurt and undermine you, it is likely these suggestions will not work. If this is the case, take comfort in the knowledge that your children will grow up knowing you were their source of safety and consistency. For the seemingly thankless hours of effort you will put in, they will learn responsibility, respect, commitment, work ethic, and a sense of security from you. This recognition will foster a lifelong bond between you and your child that will serve him or her well in future relationships.

WHAT TO DO IF . . .

Many divorcing parents I see in class or for therapy ask me for tangible suggestions for what to do if certain challenging situations occur that interfere with parenting time. The following are brief discussions on some common "what if" questions and some practical ideas for dealing with each.

A Child Refuses to Go with a Parent

Many divorcing parents encounter situations where a child refuses to go with one parent during his or her parenting time. This can be especially difficult if the child is visibly anxious or sobbing at the time of refusal.

With babies and very young children, the refusal may simply be a case of "stranger anxiety" (see chapter 7 for more information on this) or discomfort with the sudden change between two different caregivers. This is particularly true when there has been a significant lapse of time between visits with one parent.

With older children, the refusal may be based on resisting change, but they may also refuse to visit a parent if they are angry at him or her or blame that parent for the divorce. Or, they may oppose certain rules or consequences in a parent's home and therefore refuse to spend time there.

There are many ways to deal with children's refusal to visit. *Before continuing with the following suggestions, you should always explore the possibility that your children are refusing because of some sort of abuse or neglect.* If the child shows other signs of anxiety when in the presence of the other parent or when speaking about being with that parent, take note. Consider taking the child to a therapist to talk about the feelings that are keeping the child from being comfortable with that parent. A professional may be able to help the child figure out the source of anxiety and assist you and your former husband or wife in dealing with the situation.

Neither parent should overreact to a child's refusal; the parents should react with calmness and understanding, as the situation can be very hurtful to the rejected parent. That said, don't take the refusal personally; it is quite common for children to act on their discomfort by refusing a visit. Try to be sensitive to the child's feelings and tell him or her that you appreciate how difficult it must be to have to change modes so often. *Both* parents should encourage the child to go. When you both clearly support the visit, it can help the child feel more comfortable with leaving. The following is an arrangement that two parents I was treating came up with to address their child's refusal to visit.

"Christine" and "Charlie" had a three-year-old daughter, "Ava," together. Although they had never married, they had lived together since she was born. They had recently separated and Charlie was supposed to be taking Ava every other weekend. The problem was that whenever Charlie came to pick up Ava, she would cry, hide behind Christine's leg, and refuse to go with him. Charlie was getting frustrated with Christine, expecting her to just peel Ava off her leg and hand her over. Christine, on the other hand, would comfort Ava and tell Charlie to "just leave." The more Christine and Charlie argued about the transfer, the more upset Ava would get.

By the time Christine and Charlie came in to see me, they were very angry with each other and Charlie had not had time with his daughter for over a month. I worked with them to create a plan that would succeed in giving Charlie the much-needed bonding time with his daughter while decreasing the distress Ava was feeling with the visits.

Charlie came to Christine's apartment and played with Ava for a while in her own setting. After about a half hour, he attempted to coerce Ava to leave with him. She immediately refused and ran crying to Christine. Then, Christine and Ava drove to a nearby park while Charlie tagged along behind them in his own car. Both parents played at the park for a while before Christine prompted the idea of hide-and-seek. This gave Ava some momentary comfort with Christine's absence. Shortly thereafter, Christine excused herself to run out to the parking lot to retrieve a ball and some bubbles she had there. Reluctantly, Ava let her go but watched dutifully until Christine returned. This went on for more than an hour, with Christine eventually being able to drive away for fifteen minutes to fill up her tank at a local gas station. Each time Christine left, Ava became slightly more comfortable with the lack of her presence. Ultimately, Christine was able to leave the park and return home without a single tear from Ava.

During the couple's discussions in our sessions, Charlie was able to see that Christine did, in fact, support Ava going with him. She had just become so frustrated and confused in figuring out what to do that it was easier just to send Charlie away than it was to find a solution to Ava's anxiety. The couple was initially stuck with not having a solution to Ava's refusal to go with Charlie. But they were able to create a relatively simple plan that desensitized Ava to Christine's absence and fostered a relationship between father and daughter.

Keep in mind that simply not liking Mom's or Dad's rules is not a good enough reason to avoid spending time with a parent. It is very important that *both* parents support this. If your child is refusing to go with one of you because he or she doesn't want to go to bed at a certain time or doesn't want to miss a movie, both parents should insist that the child still needs to go.

Likewise, if your child is refusing to go with one parent because he or she is mad at the parent, it's not okay to cut off that parent completely from the child's life. There is an important life lesson in working through anger and disagreements with others rather than just avoiding them. Obviously, as children get older (and bigger!) it may be impossible to *force* them to go with a parent. It is important, however, to keep encouraging the visits and facilitating arrangements where a parent and child can connect or interact with each other.

A Child Misses the Other Parent

It's completely normal and natural for children of divorce to miss one parent while spending time with the other. It's important that parents recognize this and allow their children to express their feelings of sadness over missing the other parent.

You can normalize your child's feelings by saying, "I know it must be hard to not see Daddy all weekend." Then, follow up by encouraging the child to find an outlet for his or her emotion. Persuade the child to color a picture or write a letter to the parent he or she is missing. Keeping a diary is a great idea; the child can write about feelings or record events to share with the missing parent when they are together again.

You can also allow the child to call the other parent at work for a quick hello or to leave a message on the parent's voice mail at home. Be aware that if the child is not allowed to contact the other parent while not with him or her, this may increase the anxiety the child experiences and may end up being the reason for refusing a visit.

For younger children, keeping photos of the other parent handy or having the child bring along some favorite books the other parent reads with him or her can be very comforting when a child misses a parent. Because some young children have difficulty with the concept of time, you can make a calendar accessible so that they can monitor when they will see the other parent again. Some divorcing families I've worked with use bright color coding (with markers and stickers) to make the days and times with each parent very clear.

A Child Manipulates or Lies to Parents

Older children and teenagers are notorious for using manipulation tactics with their parents. When there are two separate housing arrangements and parenting experiences, children can attempt to pit their parents against each other in order to manipulate any given situation. One family I saw for therapy provides a perfect example of how a child of divorce can try to "play" her parents.

"Gretchen" was a nine-year-old girl whose parents had been divorced for almost one year. Her parents, "Annette" and "Lucas," shared custody. Gretchen showed up at Dad's house with thirty dollars she said she earned by doing errands at home. She asked her dad to take her to the store to buy a new DVD she wanted, and Dad agreed.

Later that evening, Annette called to tell Lucas she thought Gretchen had stolen money from her purse—a ten-dollar bill and a twenty-dollar bill, to be exact. Lucas asked Gretchen about it and initially she denied taking the money. Eventually, though, she admitted stealing the cash from her mother. Annette and Lucas discussed the situation and decided that the new DVD Gretchen had bought would be taken away until she had earned back the money she had taken.

A week later, Gretchen returned to Dad's house with thirty dollars in hand. She explained that she had earned the money doing chores around the house. Lucas then gave Gretchen the DVD, which she proceeded to watch right away. A few days later, Lucas found out from Annette that Gretchen had yet again lied; she had not earned a penny from doing any chores or housework.

It's obvious from this scenario that Annette and Lucas could have saved themselves from the situations with Gretchen had they prioritized having a follow-up conversation regarding the lying and stealing issue. The key to avoiding being manipulated by your child is *frequent communication between parents.*

Additionally, both parents should discuss appropriate consequences for lying and stealing, and both should stick to upholding those consequences. In the case of Annette and Lucas, they decided that each parent should choose an independent consequence for each of their homes. Lucas grounded Gretchen from all TV and computer time for two weekends at his home for lying to him and for coercing him into allowing her to buy something with stolen money. Annette chose to have Gretchen do additional housework and chores and to donate all the allowance money she earned from that to a local animal shelter.

A Child Is Irritable Upon Returning from a Visit

For children of divorce, there is inevitably a different "feel" to the time spent at either parent's home. Parenting styles; house rules and consequences; the amount of yelling, disorganization, and chaos in the home; people and activities present; and the amount of sleep and downtime may all differ greatly between the two homes. These inconsistencies often require some adjustment by the child as he or she reenters one household after leaving the other one.

Some parents describe their children being "off the wall" when they return home after spending time with a parent who is less structured and more easygoing. Other children cry, are irritable, or show more defiance upon their shift from one environment to another. Some children will act out physically against a parent or test the boundaries each time they return home.

There is some adjustment required of *all* human beings when they move between differing environments. For instance, compare your work setting with your home setting—most people make some changes in their behavior when entering either of these surroundings. Children are no different; however, they often lack the cognitive ability to make sense of this need to change. Therefore, many children of divorce will struggle a bit with adapting to the varying confines of each home.

There are a few ways to deal with the irritability children may experience upon returning home after spending time with the other parent. If at all possible, allow some transition time when your child first arrives back home. Have a snack or meal prepared, have the child's favorite movie playing on the TV, or sit down to play a board game or color with him or her. These activities are less structured than engaging in more demanding tasks such as doing homework, cleaning a bedroom, or running out to do errands.

When your child is irritable, try not to respond with matching touchiness. Calmly tell the child that he or she needs to take a little time to adjust to being back home. In extreme cases, you may need to send your child (gently) for a time-out or to his or her room to cool off. Let your child know that you understand the difficulty in getting used to new rules and surroundings again.

Sometimes, overlapping mom time and dad time can help children adjust to the change. For instance, as a close to Dad's weekend, he might consider bringing the kids back to Mom's house and then staying there for dinner to help the transition go more smoothly. Also, giving the children a little warning that the transition will be happening soon can help prepare them for the upcoming change. You can say something like, "Hey, kids—another half hour of playing and then we need to get packed up and ready to go back to Dad's house. I'm sure Dad's got dinner going and is looking forward to seeing you guys."

The transition will certainly be easier on your child if you both refrain from arguing during drop-off and pickup. Try to be polite and respectful to your ex-spouse, and do not discuss potentially hot topics during these transition times. Attending to these factors can help children make the transition between Mom's time and Dad's time a bit less stressful.

One Parent Lives Far Away

Sometimes, after a divorce, a parent may relocate far away from where the children reside. Obviously this situation makes for minimal parenting time with the parent who has moved away. However, there are several ways that you and your former spouse can stay involved in a child's life from afar.

Some distant parents expect children to stay with them during school breaks or summers. This does not always work. It can be difficult for a child to leave the parent, home, friends, and life he or she is used to for the other three-quarters of the year. Even if the child agrees to go off with that parent for a month, sometimes the child *and* the parent end up disappointed with the visit. It can be tough for a parent and child to reengage readily if they have had minimal contact for a long period of time. Don't be discouraged. In time, both child and parent will begin to re-create their relationship, albeit not always the same one they had before.

If you are a distant parent, you should plan on being in touch with your child as frequently as possible. Continued growth in the technological world offers countless ways to do this. You can send e-cards, text, FaceTime, or join other social media sites, like Facebook, Snapchat, or Instagram, to stay involved with your child. Some parents will even go "old school," sending fun letters with decorated envelopes. You should make every effort to receive school reports and pediatrician-appointment feedback so you are up to date with what's going on in your child's life. You should plan on sharing your life with your child as well, sending photos of your home or pet or recent vacation.

You can also help foster a long-distance relationship with your child by creating unique rituals between you. To your teenage daughter or son, perhaps you can send along a favorite CD mix or a book by a beloved author.

One divorced dad I saw for therapy sent his son an online "candy bar quiz" because they had been discussing what their favorite candy bars were during a recent phone conversation. The son gloated after taking the quiz because he had correctly identified sixteen out of the twenty candy bars by viewing cross-section photos of the insides of them. Dad, on the other hand, had chosen only seven of the candy bars correctly.

Another long-distance parent and her fourteen-year-old son sent an empty journal back and forth to write about what was happening in their lives. For younger children, a long-distance parent can design a weekly questionnaire they both fill out and share with each other. Some sample questions might include "favorite color," "yuckiest food," "dream vacation spot," "If you were an animal, which one would you be and why?" or "What book are you reading right now?"

The nondistant parent plays an important part in fostering a relationship between the child and the parent who has moved away. Many parents harbor anger and resentment toward the distant parent and may show this by saying negative things about his or her choice to move away. Hearing these disparaging remarks can set a child up to feel negatively about the distant parent, leading to a deterioration of the relationship between the two. Even if you are angry with the other parent and want to punish him or her, remember that by expressing this aloud, you are hurting your child. Regardless of your feelings about the move, it is better to support your child's relationship with the distant parent. Help the child remember the other parent's birthday and encourage the child to write to the parent and to call to share any exciting news. Talk about favorite holiday memories and fun times the child shared with the distant parent.

TWO IMPORTANT RULES OF PARENTING TIME

I often tell parents in my divorce-parenting classes that there are two "Golden Rules" of parenting time that are very important to adhere to. Not only does following these rules show respect for the other parent, but it highlights to the children their right to have access to both parents. These rules help postdivorce families to create separate and different, yet equal, relationships with children at both homes.

Do Not Make Plans on the Other Parent's Time

Special events are unavoidable. However, it's a good rule of thumb to try to avoid scheduling things for the other parent's parenting time. Clearly communicate to the other parent any information about party invitations or special events that will take place during his or her time with the child. If you want to offer assistance to ensure the child can attend such an event, feel free to express this to the other parent. You can also offer to swap days or weekends if it makes it easier for the child to attend a particular function. Ultimately, though, the parent on whose parenting time the special activity falls should make the decision about whether a child can attend. *Never* show up at the other parent's door with a laundry list of things you have planned or want accomplished.

Do Not Take Parenting Time Away as a Punishment

Spending time with *both* parents is a child's *right* and should not be used as a reward or punishment. Some children will manipulate this to try to get out of doing something at one house by going to the other. It is not appropriate to tell children that they may not go with another parent *because* they have not cleaned their rooms or completed homework. It is, however, completely appropriate to tell a child that he or she will not be able to go with the other parent *until* he or she has completed a particular chore. You might call the other parent and explain the situation, hoping the parent will support your decision and encourage the child to follow through so that their weekend together can begin.

LIMITED PARENTING TIME

There are several reasons why a parent may have very limited time with his or her children after a divorce. Perhaps a parent lives far away and can only see the children for a weekend every three months. A job that entails a great deal of travel may disrupt regular parenting time for yet another parent. In other instances, divorced parents remarry, have more children, and get caught up in their "new" families, thereby reducing the frequency of parenting time with their first set of children. And yet other parents engage minimally with their children postdivorce because of their own mental health, substance-abuse, or legal issues.

Ideally, all divorced parents would continue to have regular contact and involvement with their children. However, if this is not the case for one of the aforementioned reasons, you should strive to increase the quality of what little time you spend with the children. Strong, positive, healthy relationships between parents and children are key to the security and comfort of children postdivorce. The following is a good example of a dad with very limited time to offer his kids who was able to make a meaningful relationship with his three children after a nasty divorce.

"Jim" went through a very difficult divorce and was left unemployed and practically penniless after the drawn-out process. He was unable to find another job locally and had been evicted from his apartment. His brother offered to let Jim move in with him and do construction work at his company. The only problem was that Jim's brother lived several states away.

Jim ultimately accepted his brother's offer and moved away shortly thereafter. He arranged to rent a car and drive home every other month to be with the children (ages 6, 8, and 9) for an overnight. He would drive the eight hours on a Saturday, get a hotel for himself and the kids for that night, and return them to their mom the following morning. Jim's ex-wife was agreeable to this arrangement because, without a computer and only a cell phone, contact between the children and their father had been minimal.

Jim had limited funds and needed to be creative with how to reengage with his children during the time he was able to spend with them. With the money he spent on the rental car, gas, and hotel, he couldn't afford to take them anywhere really spectacular.

Jim came to me with feelings of low self-worth and depression due to his inability to be involved with his kids on a regular basis. He also felt bad that he couldn't buy them the toys and fun things they liked.

Jim and I spent some time focusing on the individual needs and special interests of each child. Then we explored ways in which he felt he could contribute to each child's life. Jim was able to acknowledge that his lack of involvement with the children was only temporary, as he was trying to work and save money to be able to afford to move closer again.

Jim spent a tremendous amount of time and effort putting together what his children would later call "Daddy's Surprise Trunk." He described to me with great pride and excitement how his children had loved his first visit with them.

"Well, first I picked them up and told them about my trunk idea. We opened it up and looked inside. I had brought along a plastic baseball bat set and packed a big picnic basket and blanket. We went to the park for the afternoon. I brought along a cheap loaf of white bread to feed the ducks and I borrowed some sidewalk chalk from my brother's kids. We played with a Frisbee and had lunch. I had a notepad and pen and asked the children to each teach me something they were learning in school. I had done up a twenty-questions list for each child—I asked them what their favorite food was, who their favorite friends were at school, who their least favorite teacher was and why, and what was the best/worst thing that had happened to them that week.

Then I surprised the kids with free passes to a laser light show at a planetarium nearby. They even had free cookies and brownies afterward. I had also called the local library beforehand to see what was going on the weekend I was coming up. Before bed, we all spent about an hour telling all sorts of stories about what had been happening in our lives. My nine-year-old told me about having his first cavity filled, my eight-year-old told me about a boy at school who had a crush on her, and my six-year-old told me about a bully at school. I helped them figure out what to do about these situations. And to help out my ex-wife when I dropped them back off, I talked to them beforehand about what they could each work on doing better around the house to help out Mom or be better behaved. I can't tell you how good I feel about this past weekend."

PRACTICAL IDEAS TO HELP PARENTING TIME GO MORE SMOOTHLY

Parenting time is meant to be a positive, relationship-strengthening experience for both the parents and child. Nothing is more disappointing (to the parent *and* the child) than when the time spent together is rushed, disorganized, and stressful. What follows are a few practical suggestions for helping things go smoothly during your parenting time.

Plan Ahead

Parenting time will inevitably go more smoothly if you plan ahead. This can include arranging your work schedule to accommodate more flexibility when you will have the kids in your care and doing errands and catching up on cleaning during off times with them. Cooking and freezing extra meals when you have opportunity and keeping them handy to reduce the time you'll need to be cooking will also increase the quality time you will have with your kids.

Respect the Other Parent's Time

To make parenting time easier for each other, you and your former spouse need to respect each other's time. This means, for example, not trying to switch times or cancel taking the kids at the last minute without a good reason. When doing this, a parent sends the message that the other parent's time and plans are unimportant.

Get Organized

Being organized can help you better manage the job of single parenting as well. Spend some time attending to your home's setup. Have you arranged the drawers so that young children can put away clothes into distinct categories like underwear, pants, and pajamas? Is there adequate storage for toys and other kid stuff? Is there a routine in place for packing up backpacks, lunches, and after-school sports equipment the night before school? Taking some time to organize your home can go far in terms of organizing your life as a single parent.

Let Go of the Notion of Perfection

No parent can do everything, and single parents are no exception. The more quickly you can let go of the notion of perfection, the more quickly you'll be able to enjoy the time you have with your children. Try not to stress if you haven't put away the clean laundry for over a week or the kitchen floor is sticky and full of crumbs. If you haven't been able to exercise in two weeks or are two months late with thank-you notes from Christmas, it's not the end of the world.

Attempt to set realistic goals for yourself. Consider making a prioritized to-do list and tackle one or two things each week until you've accomplished everything on the list. Give yourself a break—single parenting is tough and perfection is not necessary to have a meaningful, healthy relationship with your children.

When in Doubt, Ask the Other Parent for Suggestions

If you find yourself struggling with certain components of the single-parent rigmarole, don't be afraid to ask the other parent for suggestions. Asking for help is not a sign of weakness, but rather a wise way to help you parent your children. Perhaps Dad is experiencing difficulty in getting all the kids settled down at bedtime. If he asks Mom how she manages it, she might have some suggestions for how she successfully conquered the issue a number of months prior.

Allow Comfort Items and Toys to Travel with Your Children

It's important to allow your children to bring their comfort items and favorite toys back and forth between their homes. This not only eases a child's transition between the two settings, but it also allows him or her to feel more "at home" at both places. There's nothing more disappointing to a child than when one parent buys a new video game or toy and then does not allow the child to take it to the other parent's home.

Some parents keep a separate set of *everything* at each of the children's homes. This is certainly not necessary, nor is it advisable. It is, however, a good idea to keep "extras" at each home—common items such as toothbrushes, baby "binkies," notebooks, art supplies, and spare sets of clothes in case the child forgets something.

Don't Overspend or Overindulge Your Children

To make parenting time with your kids less stressful, try not to overspend or feel pressured into indulging your children while they are with you. Children need quality time and a connection with a parent far more than they need material things.

There are many inexpensive or free things to do with kids. A family outing need not include amusement parks and restaurants. Picnics, hikes, ice skating, fishing, going to the beach, and attending free concerts in the park are great ideas for family bonding. Local libraries carry any number of free family passes to local zoos, aquariums, or museums. You can simply check them out with a valid library card. Search the local newspaper for other free area events to attend with your children.

Make Your Home Comfortable

A home that is child friendly can help divorced parents and their children feel more comfortable while they are there. Things will go more smoothly if there are no child-safety concerns and the house setup is conducive to the entire family's needs. Things like having hand towels at a child's level and step stools in central places keep everything running more seamlessly in a busy household.

Keep the Other Parent Updated

To ease the single-parenting job for both Mom and Dad, be sure to update your ex-spouse on any important changes that may have occurred while your child was with you. For example, it would be helpful to let your ex-husband know that before your son showed up at his house for the weekend, he had a detention at school that week or that he had some problems with a bully. Likewise, occurrences like a teen's traumatic breakup with a boyfriend or a recent illness are things you should tell the other parent about prior to the parenting exchange. Knowing these things may help your ex-husband or ex-wife better understand the child's mood or behavior.

* * *

Parenting time is the most important thing you can give to your children. Keeping the aforementioned things in mind, it is possible for you to set up low-stress and high-bonding time with your children that will help bolster them against many of the negative effects of divorce and the ups and downs of life in general.

5

QUESTIONS THAT DIVORCING PARENTS ASK

I devote about a quarter of my six-hour divorce-parenting class to addressing the questions and concerns of class participants. Here are some of the most common.

WHEN ONLY ONE PARENT IS HELPING CHILDREN COPE WITH DIVORCE

Q: How am I supposed to follow all the advice I hear from experts on how to help my children cope with our divorce if my ex-spouse isn't willing to cooperate with doing these things?

A: In some divorces, the responsibility of emotionally supporting the children throughout this traumatic time falls on one parent. This can be one of the most difficult parts of the divorce. Children soon learn that the treatment they receive from each parent will be different, as no two parents are exactly alike. If only one parent is approaching the discussions and issues surrounding the divorce in an appropriate manner, there's not a lot you can do about it.

Extreme cases, where one parent is causing the children psychological or emotional agony and pain, may warrant legal intervention. A parent can file for a restraining order, ask the court to reduce the time spent with that parent, or request supervised visitation. Sometimes parents may need to resort to these methods in order to prevent further damage. But unless the situation is severe, it's best for parents to allow children ample access to both of them, even if one parent is not handling the divorce in what the other believes is a gentle and sensitive manner with the children. Children quickly recognize which parent is helping to ease their pain and which parent is contributing to it. They also learn different things from each parent; perhaps the child learns resiliency and responsibility from the way Dad deals with the divorce, and selfishness and anger from Mom's reactions and behaviors. Experiencing this range of (not always so nice) responses is unfortunate, but it is also a minicourse on the real world. If at least one person is parenting the children in a healthy manner, this person can help them develop ways to cope with the poor responses of the other parent.

Naturally you want to protect your children from any negativity or emotional pain. However, this is impossible. Sad situations and unexpected traumatic events can occur at any time. The old adage "Life is unfair" holds undeniably true. You cannot fully protect children from the pain of life, and the pain of divorce is no easier to protect against, especially when one parent is not particularly invested in doing so, even for the kids' sake.

In a child's early years, kisses and Band-Aids frequently make boo-boos feel better. But as children grow older, such easy interventions for solving their problems are far less effective. Nevertheless, don't doubt for a minute that in the wake of a divorce caring actions can have the same power in healing hearts as a bandage does in patching up a scraped knee.

Although one parent cannot control his or her ex-spouse's actions (or lack thereof), he or she can work daily to ensure that the children's experiences with the ex-spouse will be happy and healthy ones. It's important to channel any frustrations in a healthy way. You can turn those frustrations into your own commitment to work patiently and diligently through your divorce with your children's best interests in mind and at heart.

(FAILED) MARRIAGE MEMORABILIA AND CLOSURE

Q: My husband and I have just finalized our divorce. Recently, my ten-year-old daughter asked to see my wedding dress and albums. I'm concerned that seeing these things might make my daughter sadder and wish that we were back together. Should I let her? I

**stuffed them way in the back of the attic many months ago and
really don't want to look at them. Frankly, I'm also afraid of my
own feelings about bringing out these items.**

A: The short answer to the first part of this question is *yes!* By all means,
give your daughter the access to what she wants to see. I've seen many
divorcing parents in therapy over the years, and in my experience there
are many ways that ex-spouses choose to have closure at the end of
their marriage. Some simply destroy or get rid of all memorabilia from
their failed relationship. In this case, there are no wedding mementos
to share with the children.

However, if you haven't gotten rid of your dating and wedding
keepsakes, then please *don't*. Looking at wedding memorabilia and
proof of happier times can be a tool for healing, as well as provide a
sense of closure—for both you and your children.

Not only is it important to let your daughter see wedding items if
she's interested, but also to offer honest responses about any questions
she may ask (e.g., "Were you in love with Daddy?"; "Was there ever a
time you didn't fight?"; "Were you happy?"). Children of divorce need
affirmation from their parents that the concept of commitment and
marriage is not a complete sham. They need to know there were wonderful moments, reasons you thought you could make a life together,
and good times and experiences you won't ever forget or regret. Most
marriages have had some of these things, at least at some point. Children need to grow up knowing they can take a chance on commitment
rather than avoid it for fear of experiencing the tragedy they witnessed
between their parents.

As for your concern about your daughter feeling sad, remember
that sadness is part of most children's experience with divorce. It's like
an open-casket wake in some ways; although quite painful and sad to
view the deceased in the coffin, for many people this helps with closure. If your daughter is asking to see your dress and photos, there is a
reason. It is important not to deny her curiosity or needs; be there to
support her and answer any questions she might ask.

The second part of the question (regarding your own feelings about
wedding items) is a bit more difficult to address. If keeping these items
makes you uncomfortable, store them with a close friend or willing
family member. But remember that your feelings about the divorce will
undoubtedly change over the next few months and years. There may

be a time when you will want to look at these items again. If you've destroyed them during the highly emotional time of divorce, they're impossible to get back.

I asked a recently divorced client whom I'll call "Carol" to bring in her wedding album to a therapy session. She looked at me as if I had two heads. I explained that I'd noted how she worked very hard at "holding back," that she changed the direction of our dialogue any time she started to get choked up and avoided talking about how truly devastated she was that her husband had left her. Carol had been trying to be strong and stoic and wasn't giving herself permission to feel sad or to cry. She had not begun to mourn the loss of her relationship.

She did bring her photo albums to our next session, however. Although she looked nervous about her decision to bring them along, a few minutes later she was flipping through each leaf of the album feverishly pointing out people and telling stories. Her reactions included laughter, tears, frustrated screams, and reminiscing gazes. By the end of our session, Carol reported feeling far less fearful of looking back and much more confident about her ability to feel the sadness and pain that accompanied those memories.

I also had a forty-something woman in my divorce-parenting class (I'll call her "Tracy") who came up to me after class in tears. She explained that her mother had passed away a few months before. Her mother and father had been divorced since she was a baby and never spoke to each other again or were ever present in the same room. When Tracy went down to Florida to clean out her mother's condo after her passing, she was shocked at what she found.

In the back of a linen closet was an old cigar box. Inside the box were love letters from her father to her mother. Other contents included photos of the two and wedding mementos like an age-yellowed garter belt and a passbook from their first bank account together. Tracy reported that the findings still traumatized her, and she could just not seem to come to terms with this evidence of a relationship she never knew of. She felt angry that she had been denied access to a very real part of her parents' lives, and she pored over the photos that showed smiles and endearing glances she had never seen on her parents' faces before.

There is yet another reason to hold on to old wedding memorabilia and good memories and let your children have access to them. Many children of divorce remember only the tail end of their parents' relationship (the part that was often volatile or estranged). Unless parents tell and show them otherwise, children have no reason to think their parents' marriage was ever anything but bad.

There's evidence that suggests adult children of divorce may experience less trust and happiness in their own marriages and have a higher rate of divorce than adults who grew up in intact homes. There's also research indicating that adult children of divorce experience higher rates of aversion to marriage and to having children, because they may see them as roadblocks to getting out of a relationship quickly. This suggests an early anticipation of the relationship's failure.

Many adult children of divorce I have seen in treatment do indeed report feeling afraid of ever having to experience the relationship agony their parents endured. In fact, this is also one of the reasons that divorced parents experience such high failure rates in subsequent relationships. When a person has been through a difficult and agonizing marriage and divorce, it is likely he or she will bail out of the next relationship much more quickly when the first signs of stress appear.

Keeping wedding items and having a willingness to share and discuss these objects and memories with children can be an important part of their healing. Making these objects accessible to children can also help prevent them from suffering divorce's ill effects when they are adults. Likewise, divorcing parents should consider retaining these things for themselves in case they want to revisit them.

WHAT (AND HOW MUCH) TO TELL CHILDREN ABOUT THE REASONS FOR A DIVORCE

Q: I am divorcing my wife because she is a nasty and mean alcoholic. She is currently in rehab for two weeks. When we told the children, they began to ask about why we were getting the divorce. I was unsure of what exactly to tell them.

A: It's very difficult to decide what *exactly* to tell your children about why you and your spouse are divorcing. The most important thing to consider is the age appropriateness of the information you give your children. For example, when speaking with very young children, you need to ascertain whether they even understand what the word *divorce* means. The first step in explaining your situation should be thinking about the language and specific words you will use. You may want to run your explanation by a few trusted adults first to have them offer feedback on your wording.

Most small children will certainly not understand the meaning of *alcoholic*. Some parents use the word *illness* to describe alcoholism or a mental disorder. However, the reality is that you are probably not divorcing your wife just because she is an alcoholic. It's more than likely that your wife's alcohol addiction includes verbal abuse, neglect of the children or the home, an inability to communicate well, and violent actions, all of which result in social scrutiny and embarrassment, degradation, or loss of motivation, job, or trust. These are the true issues at hand.

The following are some guidelines for telling your children about why you are divorcing.

Don't lie. Lying to your children will only foster future mistrust. Children need to know why you are divorcing. If you don't make it clear to them, they may come up with their own reasons for the divorce, and most often their assumptions will be inaccurate. One of the most detrimental conclusions they may come up with is that the divorce was their fault.

If your children have witnessed their mom's drinking and behavior changes, it's important you address that piece of it. But sound judgment is vital in deciding how much information the children need to have. You don't have to offer it all up front, but rather leave your explanation open for questions.

Also, don't be afraid to tell your children that you need a few minutes to think before answering any question.

Select your words carefully. Language is tricky business. You must be careful *never* to disparage the other parent in your explanation to the children. For example, your children will likely interpret statements such as "Your mom's a nasty alcoholic" or "You know your mom has had a lot of problems the last few years" quite differently than an adult would; a child may hear these statements as "Mom is bad and the cause of the divorce." This may cause him or her to either worry about Mom or side with you *against* Mom. Either outcome produces unnecessary emotional pressure the child does not need. Consider reframing your statement like this:

> I know you have seen all the fighting that has been going on between your mom and me lately and it sure hasn't been easy on any of us. One of the things you've seen is that when Mom and I have a fight, it's usually because Mom has been drinking a lot. When a person can't stop drinking and becomes mean

and violent when she drinks, she is what we call an alcoholic. Sometimes it's hard to trust that person anymore. I can't change Mom, and I'll never give up trying to help her, but sometimes you just can't stay in a marriage when you have very different thoughts about things like hitting someone else or using alcohol that way.

Reassure your children. If your wife is currently in treatment for her alcohol addiction, emphasize to your children that she is safe and getting help. Let them know you'll make sure they are cared for while Mom is away. Talk about all the things you have in place to help them—such as lawyers and a court to help work out money to pay for all their needs and to ensure plenty of healthy parenting time with Mom. Don't be surprised if your efforts do not seem to relieve your children's concerns, however. It's important to be honest with your children about how the change of a divorce is scary, unsettling, and full of many emotions.

HELPING CHILDREN WHEN ONE PARENT HAS A HARD TIME HANDLING THE DIVORCE

Q: I recently filed for divorce from my husband (who does not want the divorce). I think we did a pretty good job of telling our children. We were calm and explained that we would both be sure they were safe, had their needs met, and that we'd continue to look out for their best interests. However, since then, my husband has been so angry and argumentative that I think the children have been very upset by the change in his attitude.

A: A divorce is difficult for *all* parties involved. The truth is that some parents handle the trauma of divorce better than others. It sounds as if your husband began with good intentions but has been recently overwhelmed by his own feelings and frustrations. It's impossible to shelter your children from their father's emotions. Be comforted, though, that they will actually learn something about human nature and about ways of handling anger and stress.

The most logical place to begin improving this situation lies in working on good communication with your husband. The two of you must find a way to talk with each other privately about concerns and feelings. Your husband's anger is spilling out into full view of the children. You two must find a more appropriate forum to argue, whether it's with a therapist, a divorce mediator, or even a trusted friend or family member. Be sure this person can be neutral. You need someone who won't take sides, but rather who will help you both with validating real emotions and keeping yourselves on track in moving forward with your lives with minimal stress for the children.

I recently counseled a divorcing couple who agreed to bring along the husband's sister to sessions. The sister's intent was solely to help the couple get through this angry and painful time. Her role was to take notes of what each person was asking for during the meetings, and to ask for clarification when necessary. At the end of a session, she would provide the couple with a rough "contract" of agreements. The couple would look through the list, pick items they agreed on, and focus on doing them during the week. For example, one statement said:

> "Rick" feels verbally attacked when "Dana" speaks to him. Dana won't try to challenge Rick when she has a concern but will instead use calmer questions to get the information she's looking for. She also agrees to not use the terms "idiot," "bastard," "fuck-up," or "useless piece of shit" when speaking to Rick.

Dana had requests for improvements from Rick as well. Rick then chose one area he felt he should work on from the list and agreed to the following:

> Dana would like Rick to stop asking the children for information about her life. Rick agrees to ask Dana directly about any questions or concerns he may have regarding whom she might be dating or having over to the house.

The couple inevitably disagreed on some items. For example, Rick would not agree to refrain from calling the kids during Dana's parenting time. He was, however, amenable to avoid calling them during mealtimes or after 7:00 PM (the bedtime rush) when the children were at Dana's house. Nonetheless, they eventually worked out many of the items on the list, to the direct benefit of the children, who got to experience far less friction between their parents. Usually, spouses can hear suggestions better from someone *other* than their ex-spouse. The words of the former spouse will always be tainted by their (often unhappy) history together.

It's also important to remember the old adage "Children learn by example." If anger and fighting become commonplace in your household, you may discover an escalation in your children's emotions and behaviors as well. Children are notorious for pointing out their parents' poor behaviors in an attempt to justify their own. ("Why am I in trouble for punching the wall? Dad does it!") It will be important to address limits and boundaries for behavior for your children. You will also need to explain that just because a parent acts out angrily, this does not mean that it is an acceptable and appropriate display. If trouble with such behavior persists, your family would most likely benefit from therapy. In many instances, a child's displays of anger are retaliation for the pain he or she feels. For this reason, *one or both parents* may not be effective in stopping the anger cycle and boundary testing with their children; they should consult a trained professional.

Finally, *don't make promises to your children you cannot keep.* If you tell your children you will always love them and will work through the divorce while taking their feelings into consideration, they will take your words literally, and if you don't follow through with what you say, it can have a profound effect on them. If you find yourself acting in direct opposition to what you've promised your children, make sure to address it with them. Explain that you've been feeling overwhelmed and offer an apology for expressing your anger in ways that have been less than stellar. Perhaps most important, *try harder to find more appropriate outlets for emotional expression.*

WHEN CHILDREN DON'T AGREE THAT THE DIVORCE IS FOR THE BEST

Q: With all the fighting between my husband and me over the last year, I was certain the children would be relieved when we told them about the divorce. I've tried to tell them how much better things will be soon, but I can't seem to get them to believe this!

A: Although the finalization of the divorce may seem like a much-needed end to the fighting in the family, you may be surprised to discover that it does not always signal the termination of family stress. In fact, sometimes there can be an *increase* in hostility between parents when they begin their solo-parenting attempts and adjust to their new arrangements, relationships, and roles as single parents.

Let's say Dad had always been the disciplinarian in the family and now that Mom has a fair share of solo parenting time, her prior threats of "just wait until your dad gets home" don't cut it anymore. Mom has to redefine her role as a parent, create her own rules and boundaries, and implement appropriate consequences for defiant behavior.

Dad might catch wind of Mom's stricter parenting methods through his disgruntled children, who may not like the new discipline in Mom's home. Dad may then criticize Mom for her techniques and accuse her of being too tough on the children if he doesn't agree with her interventions. Mom, in turn, may stand firm on her right to parent as she sees fit, setting off yet another argument.

Another possibility is that Mom and/or Dad may feel a reduction in the amount of confrontation and a reprieve from the prior, omnipresent tension. This, however, does not necessarily mean that the children will feel the same way. Research tells us that only a few children of divorce feel relief from their parents' split. In this respect it's akin to the sad phenomenon of abused children who are removed from their parents and yet want nothing more than to return home again.

Even in the nastiest of divorces, there are still lots of good things at home. Children love their moms *and* dads. They are in their comfort zone at home—sometimes even if there is great stress there. It's scary for them to wonder what life might be like if everything changes after the divorce.

Although you may try in vain to convince your children that things will be calmer, it may take years before they are able to believe this was the best choice for all concerned. And although your children may experience less tension in the household after the divorce, they will undoubtedly experience their fair share of unwanted change and adjustment to the new family life as well.

You may not be able to control their ability to understand your choice to divorce, but as parents your choices in actions will most definitely have an impact on how positive or negative their experience will be.

WHEN ONE PARENT BEGINS TO DATE

Q: My wife and I are finally divorced. She is living with her new boyfriend and his eight-year-old daughter. When our daughters have parenting time with their mom (the boyfriend and his daughter

are always there too), I think they feel hurt because their mom always includes the other girl and splits her time and affection among the three of them. Why can't she just spend her parenting time with her own two daughters?

A: When a divorced parent enters into another relationship, especially one that includes other children, splitting time between their various relationships can become tricky. Ideally, divorced parents would spend their parenting time alone with their biological children to ensure ample time and attention for them. One would assume that these parents would then spend their nonparenting time with significant others and other family they may have. Although this sounds wonderful in theory, people rarely execute it so flawlessly in real life.

There's a saying that life goes on, and it applies to divorcing parents. During or after a divorce, many parents will get involved in new relationships and/or marriages, and stepfamilies may form. Some will enter these new relationships far earlier than others. It is normal for children to feel jealous or angry about the new setup, and others may relish the idea of new family members. Regardless of how the children feel about Mom's or Dad's new relationship, the task of dividing time between children and new relationships can be difficult.

If you are a divorced parent who has a new significant relationship and/or children, it may be difficult to put your new life on hold when your children come to stay with you. Your new romantic interest may not respond well to being ignored when your children come to visit. If there is another child (or stepchild) in your new home, he or she may have grown attached to you and may have difficulty sharing you with your biological children.

Although your children will eventually get used to the new setup in your home, there are several ways you can make it easier for them.

- If at all possible, don't introduce a new partner until the relationship is committed and serious. Also, make it a priority to talk in advance to your new partner about how you will ensure your children will be a priority in your new life.

- Create special rituals with *each* of your children. Even if it's just ten minutes of snuggling before bed each night, it becomes time that your child can count on and look forward to spending with you.

- Involve your children in planning some parts of the "new family" situation. For example, they could offer suggestions about how to split up chores or who will cook dinner.

- Prioritize attention for your children if they exhibit the need. If a child says he or she is missing you or is having a particularly difficult time with something like school or peers, carve out some alone time for him or her.

Although you cannot insist that your ex-spouse prioritize time alone with your children, you might help him or her do so by offering to give up an hour or two of your parenting time so that he or she can take one (or both) of the children out alone. Even if it's simply accompanying him or her on an errand, going for a brisk walk, or going out for a cup of hot chocolate, the time is precious.

OPPOSING APPROACHES TO PARENTING

Q: Whenever the kids spend time with my ex-wife, she puts them to bed so late that they are irritable at day care the next day. She also lets them watch too much TV and eat too much junk food. What can I do?

A: The first thing I will say is that the sooner you give up the hope of controlling your spouse's actions, the more peace you will find. When parents divorce, each adult may parent as he or she sees fit as long as it falls within a somewhat nebulous gray area of appropriateness. So if Mom chooses to feed the kids macaroni and cheese or peanut butter and jelly sandwiches for dinner every night or let them watch TV for several hours a day, there is little you can do about it. Of course, if you feel that Mom's choices are causing her to neglect the children or causing emotional or psychological suffering, you can certainly consult a lawyer or the family court. In most cases, though, personal parenting choices are allowable.

There are several things you *can* do to help the situation, however. I'm assuming you've already spoken with your former spouse about these concerns and am guessing it was ineffective. I usually advise having someone else bring up the issues with your spouse because it's often easier for a parent to hear constructive criticism that way. For example, if your day care provider has noticed your child's sleepiness, ask the person to contact your ex-husband or ex-wife about this. The pediatrician may be able to go over nutritional issues with your ex-spouse during a routine visit. And even a therapist (if one is involved with the family) may have more impact on the other parent by taking a few minutes alone to address any particular worries you may have regarding your children's well-being.

Most of all, don't give up trying! Many parents attempt to listen to a conversation if it truly hinges on their children's safety and care. Examine your technique. If you're continually saying to your ex-husband or ex-wife, "God, you feed these kids too much crap," then *stop*. That line is not working! We should never continue to do what isn't working, because it only leads to a cycle of failure and frustration. Try something more along the lines of, "You know, I've been doing a lot of research and gathering information on kids' nutritional needs and would love it if you'd agree to sit down and go through some of it with me."

One last hint: Rather than putting the focus on your husband's or wife's culpability on any given issue, include yourself in the equation as well. Make your suggestion something that you hope you can *both* talk about and work on in order to give your kids the best care possible.

If none of these suggestions improve the situation, then revert back to my original advice: *Let go of what you cannot affect or control.* I tell divorcing parents to stop themselves for a moment if they feel themselves getting worked up over their ex-spouse's behavior or choices. Getting upset over the other parent's actions or inaction is *wasted energy.* Channel every bit of your frustration into something you *can* do something about; focus that energy on your own parenting, and continue to work hard at making the best home life for your children when they are in your care.

SEX BETWEEN DIVORCING MATES

Q: My almost-ex-husband and I somehow ended up having sex the other day. Since then things have been really weird between us and we're afraid the children suspect something. Could it mean we're getting back together?

A: Believe it or not, this is not actually that uncommon. Most divorces are unilateral, meaning that one partner generally initiated the decision to split. Perhaps both parties had been unhappy and were thinking about divorce as an option, but usually one person is the first to make the move.

This leaves one person as the "leaver" and the other as the "leavee," and the "leavee" inevitably feels more victimized and wounded.

The leavee is the one who may not have been quite ready to give up on the relationship and so may feel still committed in some way to the marriage. So when a sexual moment comes along, it may be an attempt to save the relationship, to woo the other person back, or it may simply happen because the leavee still loves the leaver. I mean, come on now—who ever said that the meaning of a sexual encounter is always within a love and commitment arena? We all know better! Sex happens for a myriad of reasons. There is drunken sex, make-up sex, I-want-to-let-you-down-easy sex, making love, pity sex, obligatory sex, and the list goes on.

For many couples, the process of divorcing is an emotional rollercoaster ride. I'm not sure what was behind the sexual encounter you mentioned, but the answer certainly lies between you and your spouse. It's clear to me that you need to discuss this matter and most certainly figure out what the sexual encounter meant.

If there is "weirdness" between you and your spouse and you suspect reconciliation might be possible, then your children have probably noticed something different between the two of you as well. In therapy circles, this is a good example of the "pink elephant." In other words, everyone sees something big happening (a big pink elephant in the center of the room) but no one is acknowledging it or talking about it. It's as if everyone is pretending it isn't there. During a divorce, the vast majority of children want desperately for their parents to stay together. The slightest bit of cooperation or connection between the parents may give children the false hope that their parents will reconcile.

You might address this concern with your spouse and then be clear with the children afterward as to what's really going on. Explain it carefully, however. Writing it down first or practicing on a friend, a family member, or even in front of your bathroom mirror can be helpful. If you decide you will not be staying together, you might say something like, "You may have noticed things are a little less tense between Daddy and me lately. We're trying really hard to get through this and make it as easy as possible for everyone." If you think there's a chance you may reconcile, you might say something along the lines of, "You may have noticed things are a little less tense between Mommy and me lately. We're doing our best to work things out, but we're just not sure how everything will work out. I know this is difficult for everyone, but we'll let you know when we've figured it all out."

CHILDREN'S DIFFERING RESPONSES TO A DIVORCE

Q: My spouse and I are getting divorced and have three children together. We are concerned about our fourteen-year-old because she has become very argumentative and moody since we broke the news to her. Could this be due to the changes within our family? The other two children appear to be handling things well and don't seem affected by the news of our divorce. How can we be sure?

A: Divorce affects each child differently. Some children will not seem to react at all to the news of their parents' divorce, and others will show an immediate emotional or behavioral display. Unfortunately, there is no special pop-up thermometer (like the kind in oven-ready turkeys) that you can gently slip under your child's skin to tell you whether he or she is adjusting well to the news of divorce. To my knowledge, there is also no litmus test that turns pink or blue to let you know if your child's moodiness is due to the divorce or just to being fourteen. Don't be as concerned with the *why* part of your fourteen-year-old's behavior as much as addressing the issue promptly with her and finding her the support she needs to cope with things going on in her life. You may never find out (and your daughter may never even know herself) *exactly* what's at the root of her feelings and behaviors. It is more important that you recognize it and be willing to help her out.

There is a broad range of normal responses you may expect from your children. Some may be visibly sad or angry about the divorce, and others will act as if you've just told them you'll be having chicken for dinner.

Some children will be distracted in class, lose their academic motivation, or get lower grades. In many cases this change is temporary. I usually recommend that divorcing parents inform the child's teacher and guidance counselor (or social worker) of the upcoming family changes. Even if there is no problem evident, initiating contact with other people in your child's life opens the door for communication. A teacher won't normally call to let you know about the slightest nuances in your child's academic world unless the problems become rather serious or troublesome.

However, if you have already spoken with your child's teachers and have invited them to contact you with any changes or concerns (even small ones), they will be more likely to notify you quickly. Perhaps the school personnel will let you know that your daughter has begun hanging around with a new group of kids or that she seems to be sleepy and distracted in class. These are things that, unless they directly affect your daughter's performance at school, you will probably never learn. The more quickly you know of a problem, the sooner you can get help for your child.

Another frequent response to the news of a divorce may include not wanting to talk about it at all. Some kids will seem to shut down whenever the parents bring up the subject. This reaction makes it difficult for parents to gauge what their children may be feeling or thinking. If your child reacts in this manner, try to encourage him or her to talk with someone else about the experience. Without actually saying you'd like the child to go talk to the trusted great Aunt Mary about the divorce, you can make frequent opportunities for your child to spend time with her. Arrange outings with extended family members or trusted adult friends. If your child is willing, you can bring him or her to a children's divorce-support group or to a therapist for a few sessions. Even the wordless gesture of buying your child a diary or journal encourages the child to express feelings without being uncomfortable.

6

THE BIGGEST MISTAKES
DIVORCING
PARENTS MAKE
(AND HOW NOT TO
MAKE THEM)

Although no exact recipe exists for how to divorce without hurting the children, we do know some of the big things parents *should not do* in an effort to minimize the pain children may feel during and after the divorce process. This chapter identifies some of the biggest mistakes divorcing parents tend to make and offers better suggestions for how to manage the intricacies of the divorce process.

ENDING THE MARRIAGE TOO QUICKLY

In light of all the research that points to the many possible negative effects of divorce on children, it is a wonder that so many parents choose to file. It has been my experience that many couples file for divorce not because they really want to, but because they are *desperate for relief from the problems that have plagued their marriage.* Most divorcing parents I meet are emotionally drained and tired from trying, without success, to resolve these issues. They are usually discouraged and believe the only solution at that point is to end the marriage.

Unfortunately, most couples do not address their marital issues early on. By the time they seek out marriage counseling, many years of anger and resentment have built up and there is much negative emotion to break through before they can address the initial problems.

In order to save children from the pain and negative effects of a possible divorce, *parents should be sure they've tried every avenue before filing.* Of course there are many parents who do try very hard to save their marriages, and there are also couples who end up being much happier after a divorce. However, I encounter *many* divorcing parents who filed because they "got tired of trying" or because "he or she, [the other parent] wouldn't go to therapy."

Marriage counseling with a skilled and experienced clinician can be highly effective in improving the marital relationship and communication. Often, these improvements make the marriage bearable, thereby making the need to file for divorce no longer necessary. Further therapy can help the parents build an even healthier relationship that benefits the entire family. In the last year alone, I saw twelve couples (well into their divorce proceedings) for therapy who ultimately abandoned their divorces entirely posttreatment. If it is possible for these couples, who were so far along in their divorce processes, to work things out, imagine how many couples could save their marriage if they'd try this intervention before their relationship falls apart. *Think of how many children would be spared the agony of divorce if their parents could restore their healthy marital relationships before things get ugly.*

Although no one takes the decision to divorce lightly, on many occasions the decision to divorce comes from an overwhelming emotional state rather than from a well-thought-out point of view. Once you begin the process of divorce, rarely does anyone stop you and say, "Gee, slow down; are you sure you want to do this?" Most parents I work with neglect to see that it is never too late to turn back if both have doubts about whether they really want to end the marriage. *Be sure you've tried all avenues to improve your marital relationship before you file for divorce.* It can save your children a great deal of pain.

CRITICIZING THE OTHER PARENT IN FRONT OF THE CHILDREN

One of the biggest mistakes divorcing parents make is to criticize the other parent in front of the children. It makes children feel bad or insecure when they hear something negative about one of their parents. This is especially true if a particular child looks or acts a great deal like the parent being "put down." In fact, children who hear one parent criticize the other often gravitate (in defense) toward the parent being disparaged. *Denigrating your ex-spouse in front of the children can actually do great harm to your own relationship with the children.*

It can be quite difficult to withhold negative feelings toward the other parent, especially when the individual has said or done things to hurt the family deeply. However, it is imperative that divorcing parents learn to bite their tongues and refrain from degrading each other. The damage is far too great for children. For example, if a mother says to her child, "Don't count on him showing up anytime soon—you know you can't trust your father," the message suggests to the child that he or she is not important enough for Dad to remember. The child will learn whether this is, in fact, the case on his or her own in due time.

Even sarcastic statements or such nonverbal actions as rolling your eyes or shaking your head can convey a negative message. If you are a parent who harbors angry feelings about your ex-spouse, try to manage these feelings by venting to friends or by journaling. Likewise, address this issue with any extended family members who disparage the other parent in front of your child. Tell these family members that you would prefer they not speak that way in front of the children. Limit or monitor your children's time with any family member who cannot honor your wishes.

Children know they are products of *both* Mom and Dad, and therefore hurtful comments from one parent about the other vilifies both the parent *and* the child, who is genetically one-half that parent. *At all costs, strive to keep your children sheltered from your negative feelings about their other parent.* Take comfort in knowing that all children will one day figure out their parents' strengths and weaknesses and make their own judgments on who is deserving of their love. You need not rush this process, because in doing so, you will undoubtedly damage your own relationship with your children.

FIGHTING IN FRONT OF THE CHILDREN

Fighting in the household is something families commonly experience in the throes of a divorce. When parents fight in front of their children, they add unnecessary stress to an already difficult situation. Many children experience feelings of concern or worry for a parent they believe is being unfairly attacked, and subsequently feel they must protect that parent. This can lead to a position we call *parentification*, where a child assumes the role of a parent.

Being parentified can be harmful to a child because it does not allow him or her to enjoy childhood, but rather it forces the child to grow up too fast. The parentification of a child may interfere with normal development and functioning. Rather than being concerned about run-of-the-mill things such as homework and their social lives, parentified children often focus their energies elsewhere: listening in on a parent's phone calls, interfering in a parent's new romantic relationship, or involving themselves in feuds between Mom and Dad. These efforts detract from the time these children should be spending doing other, more age-appropriate things.

High conflict between parents during and after a divorce has an unequivocal negative effect on children caught in the middle. The conflict not only encourages parentification of children, but causes them a great deal of stress and emotional pain as well. There is no upside to the effects of conflict on children. Children often place themselves in the firing line by involving themselves in arguments that are volatile and often inappropriate. Many children grow up to resent their parent(s), who put them into this adult role by bringing the fighting into their world.

If you and your ex-spouse are prone to fighting and find it difficult to control it in front of your children, you both must agree either to meet apart from your children or to communicate solely via e-mail or voice mail. Some divorcing parents are able to come up with a signal to let the other parent know the conversation feels as if it may get heated soon. When the signal is given, both parties must agree to discontinue the conversation while the children are within earshot.

A note of caution: Be very careful about arguing with your ex-spouse when you think the children cannot hear you. Children are far more perceptive than we give them credit for and often witness fighting their parents thought they had not. *There is no such thing as too much precaution when it comes to keeping children out of their parents' arguing.*

MAKING ERRONEOUS ASSUMPTIONS

A serious mistake divorcing parents frequently make is to *assume* things about the other parent. For instance, let's take a dad who is frustrated with a mom who has given the children inappropriate information about an affair that led up to their divorce. The dad is angry and shocked that the mother would use such poor judgment in telling the children the details of the affair. The father is making the (wrong) assumption that the mother ever had the ability to gauge good judgment in the first place.

Perhaps if the father looked back in time, he might recall that the mother was the one buying beer for her teenager long before he was of legal drinking age, and then letting her nine-year-old watch R-rated movies. The father's error is in *assuming* the mother knows what good judgment is and then basing his expectations of her on this assumption. *Do not have expectations now for your ex-spouse that he or she was unable to meet before the initiation of your divorce.* It's better to work on addressing any problem areas *anew* with your ex-spouse than to build on resentment from age-old trouble spots.

Sometimes a divorcing parent *assumes* the other parent doesn't care about the children, based on that parent's choice of action or inaction. But often, parents make poor choices *not* because they don't care about their children but because they are caught up in their own emotional place. These parents often cannot see past this place to consider the best interests of their children.

Another common assumption divorcing parents make is in fully believing something a young child might say about the other parent without confirming its authenticity. Although not meaning to outright *lie*, many children embellish what they say because that it is truly what their perception of a situation is. For example, a young child may tell Mommy that Daddy "never lets me eat anything at his house." If Mom *assumes* the child is telling the truth, she might get very angry and concerned about how Dad is caring for the child. However, if Mom fleshes out the details a bit, she may find that Daddy does in fact never allow the child to eat anything in the house *except for* the three meals and two snacks he provides on the Saturdays he spends with the child. *In order to reduce needless stress between yourself and the other parent, explore things carefully before you make assumptions.*

COMPLETELY CUTTING OFF FROM A CHILD

Cutting off entirely from a child can have disastrous consequences. The feeling of abandonment that may result can remain with a child for his or her entire life when a parent disappears in this manner. They don't understand the complexities of a difficult marital relationship and divorce, and cannot help but wonder why the parent didn't care enough for them to stick around. Many children feel they weren't good enough or that they caused the parent to go away. *Parents should never put this needless guilt and responsibility on any child.* Regardless of the difficult circumstances of a broken marriage, it is imperative that parents stay in touch with their children, even if it is long distance.

The story of a man named "Bruce" and his two teenage daughters, "Candace" and "Blair," illustrates the traumatic effects estrangement has on children after a divorce.

Bruce was a newly divorced man who begrudgingly took my divorce-parenting class. Although he was silent for much of the class, he piped in during one group discussion regarding the need to stay connected to the children during and after the divorce. The participants in the class looked at Bruce with horrified faces as he spoke: "Screw that. I tried to see my daughters but they chose to believe their mother and blame me for all the problems in our marriage. Those girls let their mother poison them about me and I'm done trying. In fact, I haven't seen them in over six months now and I'm not going to. I'm moving across the country next month and they know where they can find me. They don't want to see me and hate me? Fine with me—there's nothing I can do about that. Let them come find me when they are ready."

Unbeknownst to Bruce, a colleague of mine had been seeing one of his two daughters, Blair, for several months. Indeed, Bruce's ex-wife had put a great deal of energy into "poisoning" the daughters against Bruce. However, Blair was unaware that her father had made any effort to contact her. The mother had fielded the calls and kept telling Bruce that his daughters hated him. Blair had no choice but to believe what her mother told her ("Your father doesn't love you—he doesn't even care if he ever sees you again") because Bruce stopped making efforts to convince her otherwise.

In this difficult scenario Bruce's wife was guilty of many things, but it was Bruce alone who was responsible for not trying harder to have a relationship with his daughters. When Bruce gave up, he put the unfair task of reconciliation on his daughters. *Even if the daughters continued to refuse to see their father, Bruce's continual efforts would have conveyed the message that he still cared.* Instead, unless something changes in their relationship with their father, Blair and Candace will grow up believing he did not love them.

During a difficult time like divorce, it is especially important to regard children's tender emotions with the utmost care and sensitivity. *Never abandon your child, no matter how painful it may be to stick around.* Even in cases where the child rejects you, you never know when the child might have a change of heart.

USING THE WRONG WORDS

Words are very powerful, and perhaps never more so than when a family is in the throes of a divorce. Parents must be very careful about what they say, and how they say it, to their children during this very difficult time. Never invoke threats such as, "If you don't stop talking back to me, you're going to live with your mother." Although a parent may not really intend to send the child away, these words are a powerful message that suggests the child's relationship with the parent is not secure. Another common threat—"If you don't like my rules, go live with your father and see if he can do any better"—communicates that this parent could care less whether or not the child remains with her.

During the trying time of divorce, children's emotions are often very tender. You and your ex-spouse need to be aware of this and be extra cautious about what you say to your children. Rather than saying, "God, your room is a disgusting pigsty! You live like a slob!" try to keep your words less personal and more directive. Perhaps you could say, "This room really needs some attention. Could you please have it picked up by the time you leave for school tomorrow?"

Sometimes it is helpful to remember this: Keep it simple. When addressing your child, you need not be wordy. Complaints ("I've asked you to clean up that spill a hundred times") or threats ("If you don't clean up that spill right now, I'm going to spill stuff all over your favorite things") are unnecessary. *Keep it simple.* Merely say what you mean—"Please go clean up that spill right now." If the child does not respond, just let him or her know what the consequence for that inaction will be.

Divorcing parents sometimes use complicated jargon when speaking to their children. For instance, using the terms *custody* and *child support* around young children who have no idea what these terms mean is inappropriate. This is especially true when spoken with a negative tone or energy. For example, a five-year-old boy I was seeing for therapy came into a session one day and said, "My Daddy didn't child-supported me. So he's a really bad Daddy." I asked the boy what "child-supported" meant and he responded, "I don't know but it's definitely not good."

As a divorcing parent, you need to *always think before you speak.*

USING THE CHILD AS AN INFORMANT OR A SPY

Some divorcing parents become so desperate for information about their ex-spouses that they use their children as spies. Sometimes the parent does this unknowingly by simply asking too many questions, and other times the parent intentionally sets the child up as an informant. In either case, *it is unacceptable to place any child in the role of informant or spy.*

One family I was seeing for therapy during a grueling divorce offers an excellent example of how traumatic spying can be for children.

"Carla" left "Neil" after twenty-one years of marriage. They had three teenage children together: "Cole," age eighteen; "Graham," age sixteen; and "Annabel," age fifteen. Neil was very angry and hurt by the divorce, and he was certain that Carla left him for another man. Although there was no evidence of an affair, Neil continued (inappropriately) to suggest to the children that Carla was "seeing someone on the side."

One day, Neil sat idling in a borrowed car with darkened windows outside Cole, Graham, and Annabel's high school. When they were dismissed, he called out to the kids when he spotted them exiting the building. The children were confused at why their dad was waiting for them at school because Graham and Annabel usually took the bus and Cole rode home with a friend who had his own truck. The children were even more puzzled at why Neil was driving someone else's car.

As Cole, Graham, and Annabel neared the car and could see their dad inside, they became very disturbed—Neil was dressed from head to toe in women's clothing. He wore an ill-fitting red dress, fishnet stockings, and high-heeled shoes. Additionally, he was wearing a blonde wig, clip-on earrings, women's sunglasses, and ruby-red lipstick. Before any of the children had a chance to speak, Neil signaled to them and said, "C'mon! C'mon! Get in the car! Hurry!"

The three children reluctantly hopped into the backseat of the car Neil was driving and Cole began the conversation. "What the hell are you wearing, Dad? Jesus! You look like a freak!" Annabel chimed in, "God, please tell me no one saw you here!" Graham added, "I'll freaking die if anyone sees us with you!"

Neil quickly explained that his women's garb was so he wouldn't be recognized as he snooped around outside a local motel. He had seen Carla's car parked there, and he was certain she was with her lover. He said, "We can finally prove she's been lying about this affair. I want you guys to see it for yourselves so she can't deny it or say I made it up. She's shacking up with some loser. I knew it all along! You'll see it with your own eyes!"

Despite the children's pleas to just go home, Neil parked the car outside the motel in a seedy part of town for more than an hour. He flashed the lights into various windows at the motel and asked the front desk manager if a woman of Carla's description had checked in with anyone else. The manager declined to answer Neil's questions, citing confidentiality. Finally, Neil left a nasty note on Carla's car and headed back home.

The children disclosed the scenario to me in our next session. After working through the humiliation of what had occurred, they admitted they didn't really want to see Mom with someone else if she was in fact having an affair. Graham summed it up best when he said with great frustration, "God! I'd just rather not know anything! Why can't he [Neil] understand that? Why can't he just keep this crap between him and my mom?"

I met with Neil alone at the end of the session. First, I validated his pain and his need to know. Then I explained to him that although he needed to do what he felt he had to in order to get closure on the failure of the marriage, he also needed to keep the children out of it. Although Neil had initially thought he was helping the children by giving them the proof of their mother's affair, he was able to see that perhaps the children did not crave that proof in the same way Neil did.

Sometimes you can unknowingly ask questions that make your children feel uncomfortable. Even if you do not intend to, your child may feel you are asking him or her to report on the other parent. Children of divorce will generally be more comfortable sharing information about time spent with the other parent if they are not prompted or forced to do so. Rather than asking a child, "So what did you do with Mom this weekend?" you might try saying, "So let's make a list of all the things you've done this past week and you can star a couple of your favorites." To make the mood even less pressured, try adding a little humor: "I bet doing homework will definitely be one of your favorites!"

Although it is quite normal to be curious or jealous about your ex-spouse's life and who he or she may be dating, it is inappropriate to use your child to gain information on this subject. If you're curious, call up the other parent and inquire benignly about how he or she is handling/will handle dating and introducing the children to a new person. If you're jealous, vent to a friend or to yourself on a good, long run! *Do not ask your child for information.* If you ask, "So what's Daddy's new girlfriend like?" the child usually knows the question is loaded. Although the answer might quell your curiosity, your child also knows the information may hurt your feelings or make you angry. But if the child withholds the information, he or she may be forced to lie and risk feeling guilty about doing so. This is an impossible predicament for any child.

USING THE CHILD AS A CONFIDANTE

Similar to using children as spies, some divorcing parents use their children as confidantes. Most parents who do this end up giving their children too much information. And most parents who fall into the confidante trap do so because they feel their children understand their experiences with the other parent.

For example, let's say a divorce occurred after a lengthy struggle with Mom's alcoholism and verbal abuse. Dad might say something like, "Isn't it nice to not have to have the fighting every night? You know, those fights were usually when Mom had too much to drink. I'm not sure if you noticed, but when she drank too much, she would bang stuff around and start swearing. I used to get so mad when she started that. And one time she tore my shirt even. . . ." This would be a typical way for such a parent-child confidante relationship to begin.

Some parents defend confiding in their children by arguing that they are simply using the children as sounding boards, especially if the children seem to be supportive or eager to discuss the issues brought up by the parent. Regardless of how the child reacts, much of the information will likely result in unnecessary emotional drain on that child.

Try to refrain from dumping your personal struggles and frustrations with your ex-spouse on your children—they have their own difficulties to work through and don't need to expend unnecessary energy on yours. Despite what children may sometimes say, they often *don't* really want to be their parents' confidantes but feel obligated to go along with it.

FORCING CHILDREN TO CHOOSE SIDES

One of the most detrimental situations children of divorce can be in is having to choose between parents. This puts a cruel and impossible pressure on children; it is asking them to choose which parent's feelings they inevitably want to hurt.

Sometimes the choice is straightforward, such as when one parent asks, "Whom do you really want to live with? Mommy or Daddy?" Other times the choice is couched in a less obvious, more rhetorical manner, such as when a parent says, "Isn't it just awful that Daddy doesn't even care that he is going to miss this event?"

It is important for parents to remember that forcing a child to choose between two parents does not ensure the child will express his or her true feelings and desire. In fact, many times it is just the opposite. The following is the case of a twelve-year-old girl I was seeing for therapy during her parents' very difficult divorce.

"Janelle" was an only child. Her parents, "Bev" and "Allan," were divorcing after fourteen years of marriage. Although they were battling over which parent Janelle should live with, Bev was careful never to pressure Janelle into choosing sides but was fighting in court for full custody of her. Allan, on the other hand, was continually pressuring Janelle to live with him.

One day in session, Janelle was visibly upset. I asked her what was wrong and she told me she felt "just terrible" about what she had done. She told me that she told her father that she wanted to live with him (even though she didn't really want to) just to stop him from pressuring her. Janelle figured that when it came time to tell the judge who she wanted to live with, she'd ask to see the judge alone and tell the judge the truth. Janelle said that the worst part of it was that the decision crushed her mom. She felt very bad about hurting her feelings and really guilty about lying. Janelle reported that her mom was "so cool about it" and told Janelle, "If that's what you really want and it will make you happy, I want you to go with him." But Janelle said her mom also cautioned her to "not make a decision you aren't sure of." Bev promised that if Janelle wasn't sure, she and Allan would find a way to work it all out.

After a few weeks of helping Janelle deal with her guilt and confusion, we focused on figuring out where the best place for her to live would be. Janelle wanted to live with her mom, saying she was concerned about her dad's anger and was afraid of making him mad by not wanting to live with him. I helped Janelle to role-play the ways she could tell her dad how she felt. It took her several weeks, but eventually she spoke with her father (who was initially very angry) and was able to tell him she'd rather live with her mother but see him every other weekend.

Two and a half years later, Bev is remarried and Allan has a live-in girlfriend. Janelle lives with Bev (and adores her new stepfather) and sees her dad every other weekend. Although those traumatic days of choosing between her parents are long over, Janelle still carries secret resentment toward her dad for putting her in that awkward situation. Janelle remains grateful that even though she lied and hurt her mother's feelings, Bev never made her feel bad about it or tried to pull her over to the other side.

Janelle's situation demonstrates how distressing choosing sides can be for a child. It also shows how the distress can linger when a child is forced to lie about his or her true feelings in order to appease one parent. It's important to exercise extreme caution in how you phrase things to your children. Remember that a child should never have to choose between two parents, and except in the case of abuse or neglect, a child has a right to both parents.

FAILING TO BE CONSISTENT IN PAYMENT OF CHILD SUPPORT

Not only is it illegal to avoid paying court-mandated child support, but failure to pay can also create a great deal of stress in your child. I have encountered countless children who have been directly and indirectly harmed by the lack of financial support from one parent. Along with all the other changes a child must endure during and after a divorce, failing to follow through with agreed-upon payments can demand even more adjustment on the child's part. Late child support can cause the parent who receives it to fall behind on paying bills. This can result in interest charges and late fees that, in turn, can force the parent to fall into debt. Late child support can prevent a child from registering for summer camp, getting a spot in dance class, or getting needed items for school.

If one parent agrees to pay a specific amount of money at a specific time, that parent needs to be sure it happens. If an unforeseen issue comes up, the parent needs to let the other parent know about the situation immediately and work with that parent to figure out who will cover the bills until the money is available. Not only is this a good lesson on responsibility for children, but it also sends the message to the children that the parents are considering their well-being.

Some parents play around with child support to hurt or punish the other parent. However, it often ends with the children suffering. A financially strapped, angry parent who has not received timely child support payments can be stressed out, anxious, and impatient. In this case, the parent can take out his or her suffering partially on the children, who then witness an emotionally unhealthy parent. In short, *if you have been ordered to pay child support, pay it regularly and on time.*

GIVING IN TO CHILDREN'S MANIPULATION

The definition of *manipulation* is the controlling or influencing of something, especially for one's own advantage. Many parents make the mistake of allowing their children to manipulate one (or both) of them during and *after* the divorce. It is always harder to break the bad habit of manipulation after it's been allowed to continue for a while than it is to prevent the manipulation from happening in the first place.

All children have an egocentric, or self-focused, side. It is normal for them to attempt to manipulate a situation if it gets them something they want. So if parents allow it, most children will try to make any given circumstance work out in their favor. For instance, let's take a child whose parents are divorced and whose primary residence is with his mother. As the child grows bored with Mom's 9:00 PM curfew, the child may start to complain to Mom and say that he is going to live with Dad. This may not actually be the case, but he believes that his threat may push Mom into softening her rules.

Sometimes children of divorce will try to hop back and forth between their two parents' homes when they want to avoid a certain rule at one place. Children should not be allowed to "play" their parents in this manner; the custody/living arrangement should not be thrown away just because a child doesn't like a particular rule in the household.

Letting children manipulate parents only hurts the children in the long run. When parents divorce, they often create a gap in their relationship. Living apart and beginning two new personal lives necessitates that the two parents pull away from each other. This separateness often gives a child the golden opportunity to position himself or herself between the two parents and shift the focus as he or she sees fit. Parents must be aware of this possibility and work together not to get sucked into any manipulation games a child may play.

The story of thirteen-year-old "Casey" and her parents is a good example of how manipulation works in a divorced family.

Casey's mom, "Brenda," brought her into therapy after she caught Casey with an older boy in her room one night. Brenda had returned home from a night out with friends far earlier than expected. Casey was supposed to have been at her dad's house that night but when Brenda went upstairs, she found Casey in her room with a sixteen-year-old boy from school.

Knowing that her parents had an unfriendly divorce and spoke only when they absolutely had to, Casey figured she could tell her mom she'd be at her dad's house and tell her dad she was sleeping over at a friend's house, and no one would be the wiser. Casey planned on having the boy pick her up a block down the street from her friend's house and then they'd go to Mom's house for a while because she'd be out. In fact, this plan had worked before for Casey.

In this case, Casey had learned to use her parents' lack of communication to get away with doing things she wasn't supposed to be doing. She manipulated both of her parents and the situation to benefit her own wishes. The problem was that Casey put herself in a dangerous situation that her parents were completely unaware of.

Separate houses and poor or infrequent communication are two things that facilitate a child being able to manipulate his or her parents. Although there's not much to be done about separate housing after a divorce, parents who are no longer married still need to communicate about their children often in order to prevent such manipulation from occurring.

Always strive to keep a line of communication open with your ex-spouse after a divorce. As difficult as this can be, it is imperative for the safety and well-being of your child that both you and your ex-spouse share information with each other.

FAILING TO FOLLOW THROUGH WITH AGREED-UPON PICKUPS AND DROP-OFFS

Some divorcing parents do not take their pickup/drop-off commitments seriously. It is respectful to the other spouse to follow through in a timely manner with any arrangements you have made for retrieving the children. Following through on commitments is also a valuable lesson for children to learn.

"Marybeth" and "Felix" are a divorced couple who illustrate the importance of timely pickups and drop-offs.

Felix had the kids ("Isaac" and "Hector") one weekend. He had arranged to drop them off with his ex-wife, Marybeth, at 9:15 PM on Sunday night in a local grocery store parking lot. The couple had to do pickups/drop-offs in a public place due to a remaining restraining order.

Just as Felix was getting ready to leave, Isaac and Hector began to beg him to let them see the end of a movie they were watching. After glancing at the kitchen clock, Felix agreed they could watch a few more minutes. Meanwhile, Marybeth sat in the grocery store parking lot, watching the minutes tick by, wondering where they were.

Given the rural area in which both Marybeth and Felix lived, neither had cell phone reception. Therefore, Marybeth waited until 9:35 before going into the store to call Felix. There was no answer, so she waited another five minutes before calling the police.

A police cruiser waited with Marybeth until Felix showed up at 9:50. Needless to say, Felix was angry when he saw the police car there and began an argument with Marybeth, calling her "ridiculous." Isaac and Hector were terrified by the sight of the police and worried their parents were in trouble and going to jail. The whole night was a mess.

Is ten minutes late really late? How about fifteen? Or twenty? Some divorcing parents ask me, "Don't you think my ex-spouse overreacted a bit? I was only twenty-five minutes late in picking up the kids." I have to explain that although twenty-five minutes may seem like an acceptable, "fashionably late" amount of time, that time sends a deeper message: "I don't respect your plans. My time is more vital than your time. I don't take your concerns seriously. You're not important."

Not only does not following through on pickup/drop-off arrangements show a disregard for the other parent and send a poor message about respect to the children, but it can also cause other issues. For example, one parent I counseled experienced immobilizing fear whenever her ex-husband was even a few minutes late dropping off their daughter. This was because a different ex-husband had abducted one of her other children for eighteen months. Fear of abduction, or simply not knowing where your child is even temporarily, can cause great distress for a parent.

On a simpler level, several divorced parents I have worked with have missed hair or dental appointments or been late for work due to an ex-spouse being late with child pickups or drop-offs. *If you make a commitment to take the children, always make every effort to be sure you arrive when promised, and be sure to drop them off in a timely manner as well.*

7

SPECIAL ISSUES FOR INFANTS, TODDLERS, AND PRESCHOOLERS

Even a minor event in the life of a child is an event of that child's world and thus a world event.
—GASTON BACHELARD (French philosopher and poet)

Many parents (falsely) believe that a divorce during the very early years of a child's life will not have as great an impact as if the child were older. Couples figure that if they divorce early on in the child's life, the child's experience will register only, or primarily, the separate living arrangement of the parents. However, eventually the day will come when the child will see a peer's affectionate parents and recognize the difference between the two families. As in the quotation at the beginning of this chapter, *any* event, no matter how small, has a huge impact on a child's life. Regardless of age (or any other demographic information, for that matter), *divorce affects all children on some level.*

There are unique issues that parents need to explore. Each phase of childhood—infancy, toddlerhood, and preschool—has its own specific set of features that divorcing parents need to keep in mind when considering issues such as physical custody and living arrangements. This chapter focuses on each of three primary phases of early childhood and examines the milestones and issues specific to them. Additionally, each section offers suggestions for how divorcing parents can discuss and work through the particulars of each stage in order to best care for their children.

THE DEVELOPMENTAL FEATURES OF INFANCY

Many parents believe that divorcing while a child is an infant is the best-case scenario compared with other ages in a child's life. This is simply not true. *The manner in which parents divorce is a far more important factor than the age of the child when considering the impact the divorce will have on a child.*

Infancy is a demanding phase of a child's life for many parents. It entails almost constant caregiving, interrupted sleep, and hormonal (for the mother) and emotional changes. The stress of a divorce and the subsequent demands of single parenting can be overwhelming. In many cases, the infant ends up suffering from the parent's emotional state, which may manifest itself as irritability, distress, anger, crying, yelling, or depression. Self-care and asking for help and support from family members and friends is especially important for parents who divorce with an infant in their care. The following are some of the developmental features of infancy and how divorce can have an impact on them.

Secure Attachment
The layperson's definition of *attachment* is an infant's gravitation toward and connection with a primary caregiver. The infant seeks out this particular person and prefers to be with him or her over most other people, developing a strong emotional bond. As the infant gets older, he or she may form additional bonds with other family members.

Secure attachment is generally the healthiest type of attachment a child can develop with a parent. The simplest description of secure attachment is that an infant signals distress or discomfort by crying, the parent comes and attends to the infant's needs, and the infant soon concludes this is the general way the world works. The child grows up thinking, "I'm always going to be okay—my parent(s) will take care of me and meet my needs." Children who grow up securely attached to their parents are more likely to have trusting relationships, express feelings well, and have higher self-esteem than their insecurely attached counterparts.

However, divorce can interfere with an infant's bond with his or her parent(s). If a parent becomes emotionally drained and distressed during the divorce proceedings, he or she may not attend to the infant's needs in a way that fosters that child's secure attachment. Perhaps the parent is too exhausted to respond to the infant's crying or is rough and impatient in handling and dealing with the infant. Or the parent will rely on various others to care for the child while he or she is dealing with the pressures of the divorce, making the infant irritable and distressed with the continual change in caregivers and yearning for the connection with the previous primary caretaker (the parent). These situations can all have a negative impact on the infant's ability to attach securely to the parent.

Sometimes one parent will withhold the infant from the other parent during the early stages of a volatile divorce. In these very early months of an infant's life, continual contact is necessary for the child to bond with the parent. A parent who does not allow the other parent to have access to the infant may do serious damage to that child's ability to bond with the other parent in the future.

As a divorcing parent with an infant, you need to be sure to take care of yourself during this difficult time in order to remain emotionally and physically available to offer consistent contact with and care for the child. Additionally, unless there is a serious concern of abuse or neglect, it is imperative that you *allow the infant to spend time with the other parent in order to foster the bond that naturally occurs between parent and child at this stage of development.*

Communication

An infant's first communication is through crying. This is the only method the child has for letting the parent know when he or she is hungry, in pain, or otherwise uncomfortable. Parents quickly learn to read an infant's cries and can often determine the child's message from them. The parent who spends the most time with the infant has the advantage of being able to interpret the child's cries better than a parent who does not spend time with the infant on a daily basis.

An infant is nonverbal and therefore makes sense of the world and what's going on around him or her via methods other than the spoken word. Babies and very young children closely monitor things like tone of voice, body language, and facial expressions. As babies grow, they begin to draw conclusions from the things they note about people around them. For instance, if an infant hears the mother's voice get lower and her speech become louder and more rapid (consistent with being angry and arguing with someone), the infant may feel uncomfortable and begin to cry. An infant knows that this type of talking is something he or she doesn't normally hear from the mother, and the infant reacts in a negative way to the strange sounds. *Thus, if your child is distressed or irritable, check your own behavior first. Change your behavior and, in many instances, you will find a positive change in the infant's behavior as well.*

Parents who divorce when a child is an infant must be sure to communicate often about the things they've discovered about the child's behavior and his or her comfort. Parents should share what they do to soothe the infant while in their care. It can be very helpful to a dad with a fussy infant to know that Mom rocks the child and sings certain lullabies to calm the infant. Simple things, like forgetting a pacifier or favorite blanket at one parent's house, can cause great distress for an infant. *Communication between parents is such an important part of helping an infant more easily adjust to the changes that occur when parents divorce at this stage in the child's life.*

Sometimes, when parents divorce, one parent (who may not have been involved in very much of the parenting beforehand) may suddenly be faced with the single parenting of an infant. This can be challenging to do all alone, especially when he or she doesn't have experience with infants. If the divorce is less than friendly, one parent may be reluctant to ask the other for advice or help with parenting issues. If this is the case, I strongly suggest this parent read up on this stage of a child's life and attend as many pediatric well-baby appointments as possible.

The following is a basic template you can follow in order to bolster your baby's communication skills and protect the child from the negative effects of the poor communication that often occurs during divorce.

- *Never fight in front of infants.* Just because the infant doesn't understand the words you use does not mean he or she is not negatively affected by the fighting; the tone of voice the infant hears and the tension he or she senses can be frightening to the child.

- *Always speak softly and calmly to infants.* Respond in a timely manner to an infant's cries or when he or she is notably frustrated.

- *Speak often to an infant to stimulate the child.* Babies develop language skills far before we begin to hear them talk. Also, encourage an infant's verbal sounds and babbling. This expressive "language" is how a child learns to speak.

- *Communicate to the other parent any concerns you may have about a baby who does not respond to voices or makes poor eye contact.* Catching any developmental delays early on can help your child's pediatrician formulate a plan of treatment in a timely manner.

Stranger Anxiety

Stranger anxiety is a normal developmental phase of infancy. It peaks between five and ten months of age, and it is marked by the infant's unwillingness to go to people other than his or her primary caregiver.

The occurrence of stranger anxiety can be very distressing for the parent to whom the infant is resistant, can pose particular problems to the parenting time schedule, and can often cause arguments between the parents. The following is the story of a family that exemplifies the difficulty stranger anxiety can add to a divorce situation.

"Chris" and "Lisa" were a divorcing couple sharing custody of their eighteen-month-old daughter, "Hailey." Lisa had been the primary caregiver to Hailey before the divorce because she was a stay-at-home mother while Chris worked as a high school chemistry teacher and had a side job tutoring.

Hailey was very reluctant to go with Chris when he came to pick her up for his "every other weekends." She would cling to Lisa, sometimes even crying incessantly when Chris tried to take her. Lisa had become increasingly angrier with Chris as her frustration with the situation grew. On one particular occasion, Lisa said, "Enough already! Can't you see she doesn't want to go with you? Just stop! Come in and play with her for a while, but we're not doing this anymore. She's not ready to spend overnights with you. She's trying to tell us she doesn't want to go, for Chrissakes! And all you seem to care about is what you want and you don't even care if it traumatizes her in the process."

By this time, Lisa was crying as hard as Hailey was. Chris was hurt and defensive. He said, "Just give her to me, Lisa. She's fine as soon as we leave. You're part of the reason she's like this because you won't just let go. She can sense you don't want her to. You're the one who is making it hard on her by prolonging this every time. If you'd just hand her over and leave us alone she'd be fine in a couple of minutes."

Lisa and Chris's argument ensued for several minutes before Lisa slammed the door on Chris and slumped to the floor crying. Hailey continued to cry as Chris pounded on the door saying, "I'm her parent too, Lisa! You can't withhold her from me! It might take some time for her to get used to the new setup but you're making it worse by not letting her go with me. You can't do this, Lisa. . . ."

When Lisa and Chris came to my office later that week, there was a great deal of resentment and anger between them. We worked through some of their emotion before discussing a plan for how Lisa and Chris could help get Hailey used to the new arrangement with minimal adjustment and stress.

I shared with Lisa and Chris the importance of transition time for Hailey and how a quick trade-off at the doorstep was probably not the ideal situation for her. I helped Lisa and Chris create a plan for pickup.

One hour before Chris was to arrive, Lisa was to bring out some photos of Chris and talk to Hailey about how "Daddy's coming soon." Then Lisa was to pack some of Hailey's favorite toys and tell her she would take them to Daddy's house to play with. Lisa then would play an "I-Spy" game with Hailey at the window as Chris's arrival time got closer. The two would watch and see who could spot Daddy's car first. Lisa encouraged Hailey to hide behind the door so she could surprise Daddy and say "Boo!" when he came inside. When Chris finally arrived, he was invited in for a snack and to interact with Hailey and Lisa for a while. Lisa would then walk Hailey (and her bag of favorite toys) out to Chris's car, buckle her in her car seat, and blow kisses into the air until she was out of sight. This method worked far better than how Chris and Lisa had been managing the trade-off before.

Divorcing parents should ideally keep their baby's comfort in mind when arranging pickups and drop-offs. Ensuring adequate transition time, helping the baby with adjustment to the other parent, and overlapping parenting time (with both parents present) are excellent ways to help avoid the agonizing encounters Lisa, Chris, and Hailey were experiencing.

The aforementioned setup for Lisa, Chris, and Hailey may not always be enough. If this is the case with your baby, you may need to take it one step further. Consider meeting the other parent in a neutral place (like a park or a mall) where there are many new and distracting sights. Both of you can engage the child in exploring and fun until one parent simply pulls away for a few minutes at a time to "run back to the car for a minute" (at the park) or to window shop while the other parent takes the child into a toy store (at the mall).

Stranger anxiety can make transitions between parents difficult. Divorce, and the separate living quarters it brings, can make the child's separation even more traumatic. The positive, supportive attitudes of *both* parents, coupled with taking more time with attending to the circumstances around the transition time, often help babies to have a much easier time adjusting to the change in parents.

Safety Issues

Safety issues play a big part in the parenting of any young child. Infants and babies are no exception. Common concerns include rolling off the bed or changing table, falling down (especially down steps), and choking on foods or small objects. As an infant becomes more mobile, being able to crawl or roll over, for example, concern for safety issues heightens.

Ideally, when parents divorce they should speak frequently about these concerns and remind each other of certain precautions, such as using childproof locks on cabinets that hold cleaning supplies or medicines, using plastic electrical-outlet plugs, and keeping blind cords and other dangerous items out of the child's reach. Unfortunately, many divorcing couples are less than amicable and do not want to communicate with each other. The parent who may have had less experience with caring for babies may be at a disadvantage in knowing all the current information about safety risks to small children. The following is an example of a volatile divorcing couple with an infant and how the dad's refusal to communicate ended up putting the child in danger.

"Colleen" and "Jay" had a three-month-old son, "Harrison." They were in the final stages of divorcing and had begun putting their parenting plan into action. This meant that Jay would have Harrison in his sole care every Wednesday night and every other weekend. Colleen had fought very hard to avoid Jay having any unsupervised time with Harrison, because she believed he was reluctant to listen to anything she had to say about Harrison's safety. Jay rolled his eyes at Colleen when she "nagged" him about having the car seat buckled in properly or about putting the baby down to sleep on his back. Regardless of Colleen's concerns, the court ruled in favor of Jay having ample alone time with his son and instructed the couple to communicate regularly about any special concerns or needs regarding Harrison's care.

Needless to say, Colleen was very uneasy with the arrangement and had serious concerns about Harrison's safety while in Jay's care. Colleen tried to talk to Jay early one day about a somewhat important issue she needed to share, but Jay refused. She tried to get around Jay not wanting to hear what she had to say by packing a diaper bag with detailed notes and instructions inside; she gave it to him when he picked up Harrison later that day. Jay was offended by Colleen's gesture, threw the bag into the backseat, and said, "Dammit, Colleen! Let it go. I'm a perfectly capable parent and can take care of Harrison without your help. Obviously the court thought I was fit to parent, so maybe you ought to get up to speed and leave me alone."

Later that night, Jay woke up to Harrison screaming. Jay picked him up, held him, and tried to comfort him the best he could. He tried giving his son a bottle but it was no use; Harrison was inconsolable. Jay began to worry. He thought about calling Colleen but decided he couldn't risk giving her yet another reason to think he was an incompetent parent. Forty-five minutes later, Harrison was still crying profusely and Jay thought he felt a little warm. Jay began to regret not answering the phone when Colleen had called several times earlier that evening. Maybe she knew something about this.

Jay made the decision to take Harrison to the emergency room at the local hospital, where he waited for another hour before the doctor saw his son. The doctor diagnosed Harrison with an ear infection and sent him home with a prescription for an antibiotic and some medication for the fever.

The next day, when Jay returned Harrison to Colleen, he expertly gave her all the information on when to give Harrison the antibiotic and the fever reducer and then instructed her to call for a follow-up appointment with the pediatrician in a week. Colleen listened and nodded. When Jay was finished, Colleen grabbed the unopened diaper bag that Jay had dragged in with him from the car. Colleen opened it up and showed Jay the bottle of antibiotic that needed to be refrigerated and the infant fever drops along with the detailed instructions on when to give them to Harrison. She then said simply, "I have a follow-up appointment already scheduled with Dr. Andretti for next Friday."

When I saw Jay and Colleen shortly after this encounter occurred, we worked on a plan that would leave Colleen feeling comfortable with Jay's competency and Jay feeling trusted and respected as a parent. Jay agreed to read all of Colleen's lists and take seriously her diaper bag enclosures. He promised to be open-minded and read the contents with the attitude of finding something important he may not have already known about Harrison's care. If the lists included things Jay already knew, he would simply read and then ignore them. I helped Jay to understand that Colleen's lists were really about Harrison's comfort and her own comfort with leaving him with Jay, rather than as a personal attack on Jay's abilities.

Colleen agreed to simply write the notes and lists and not "nag" Jay or make sarcastic comments about his parenting. She also agreed not to call Jay repeatedly during his parenting time with Harrison. She was only able to do this if Jay promised to call her if he had any questions or concerns about Harrison, no matter how small.

If you are not certain about all the safety concerns regarding caring for babies or have not had a great deal of previous experience, I strongly suggest reading a parenting guide on infant care. Another suggestion is to post a list (somewhere very visible, like on the front of the refrigerator) of top choking foods and ages when infants typically begin to roll over and crawl. This can be a great reminder. Also, *do not be afraid to call the other parent to ask questions about concerns you may have about the infant.* The best child care often comes from both parents working together in a respectful, child-centered manner.

The following is a list of some practical rules of thumb for making parenting time with an infant go more smoothly.

- Each of you should keep the basics such as diapers, wipes, pacifiers, onesies, bibs, and extra pajamas and stretchies at your home. It takes less time and energy to pack the bag that goes back and forth between Mom's home and Dad's home.

- If your infant or young baby has not slept away from one of you before, you may find that he or she exhibits some distress over this new circumstance. This situation can be exacerbated if the child is being separated from a mother who breast-feeds the child. In order to ease the infant's adjustment, try to introduce changes gradually and begin with frequent, shorter visits that lead up to longer (sleepover) visits with the parent.

- Caring for infants and young babies can be very demanding and time-consuming. When working out a parenting plan, keep in mind each parent's need for personal downtime.

- Both parents should try to attend pediatric well-baby visits whenever possible to ensure that they both are getting the same information and medical updates.

- Divorced parents should regularly share information on any changes that occur during their parenting time with the child. For instance, you should notify the other parent when the baby has begun to cut a tooth or rolled over for the first time. Also, if one of you discovers a certain food the baby doesn't like or has a bad reaction to, he or she should tell the other. This ensures more consistent care for the child.

DEVELOPMENTAL FEATURES OF THE TODDLER PHASE

The following is an overview of some of the normal developmental features young children face during the toddler years and discusses how divorce may interrupt or interfere with these. Additionally, this section offers suggestions for divorcing parents on how to avoid some of the dangers for children at this stage of development.

Mobility

One of the most significant changes that occurs in the toddler years is that the child becomes more mobile. Crawling soon turns into walking, and then climbing is not far behind. This immediately increases the safety risks in terms of tripping and falling. The mobility risk is enhanced by the toddler's simultaneously growing curiosity about how things work and how they feel.

Parents must constantly monitor a toddler; it can be a demanding and exhausting time. When parents divorce, communication regarding safety issues for the toddler is an absolute must.

It's essential that you and your ex-spouse examine both homes for such safety measures as toddler gates at the top and bottom of stairways, electrical-outlet plugs, and dangerous items stored out of the reach of the now-mobile toddler.

Independence and Discipline

Along with their growing mobility, toddlers also develop a newfound independence. They begin to realize they are separate entities from their parents and try to use that separateness to their advantage. Running away from the parent, refusing to do certain things, and saying no are common occurrences in toddlerhood.

When the toddler begins to act on his or her need for independence, the issue of discipline comes into play. Prior to eighteen months of age or so, discipline mostly consists of distraction techniques and saying no. As the child grows more independent, parents need more formal discipline techniques. Although it is not necessary for both parents to discipline in the exact same manner, it does make it easier for a young child if both parents are somewhat consistent in how they discipline. Time-outs are an excellent discipline option.

A child this young is capable of learning to manipulate. If you are not consistent with rules and boundaries and are not clear about your expectations of the child, the toddler can try to manipulate the situation to get the two of you to "ease off" on the consequences for poor behaviors. For example, if a toddler learns that crying or saying "sorry" results in you not enforcing a consequence for hitting a playmate, he or she will quickly learn that using these methods will help to avoid punishment. Thus, the child may go right back to hitting (not understanding that it's not acceptable behavior), fully knowing that his or her crying or "sorry" tools will bail him or her out.

There is no need to be mean or angry with toddlers; simply be consistent and enforce the rules with calmness and firmness. This sets the stage for how the child will react to disciplinary actions in the future.

When parents divorce, there is often a "tougher" parent and an "easier" parent, and the child quickly learns to try to play each parent against the other. For example, the toddler will say things like, "But Daddy lets me do it," in an attempt to get Mommy to lighten up on her rules. Ideally, you and your former spouse should speak about your beliefs in discipline and support each other's rules in order to reduce manipulation attempts.

Consistency

Toddlers love consistency. They love to read the same books over and over again, absolutely must have that last drink of water before bed, and have a particular way of eating and dunking their favorite sandwich cookies. During a divorce, when so much necessarily changes, it is important to keep things consistent whenever possible for the child.

If you can keep the same home for even a few months after the divorce or keep the toddler in the same day care facility after one of you moves, you should do so. For the comfort of the child, try not to make too many changes at once. And when changes do need to happen, focus on maintaining as many other family rituals as possible. Keep the same play dates, go to the same park, and keep the same bedtime schedule as much as possible.

Fears

Toddlers often develop fears of things such as the dark, being left alone, or dying. Divorce can exacerbate fears for young children because it can bring a lot of change and insecurity for them. Divorcing parents need to spend extra time reassuring toddlers of their love and presence.

Because toddlers do not have a good sense of time, they do not understand how long "I'll see you tomorrow" is. When the child is left with one parent for a period of time, it can be helpful to let the child keep track of the days on a calendar or draw pictures (the child eating breakfast, playing at the park, and then eating dinner) of what events will happen before the child sees the other parent again.

If a child misses or is worried about one of you while he or she is in the care of the other, parents should validate this and act on it. For instance, allow the child to call the other parent if he or she is wondering about that parent's safety. If the child expresses sadness over not being with the other parent, encourage the child to draw a picture for the absent parent or allow the child to look at photos of the other parent. *It is never a good idea to disallow any talk of the other parent while the child is in your care.* As hurtful as it can be to feel second-best, you need to understand that the child cannot control how he or she feels, and expressing feelings is an important way of dealing with these natural feelings.

Regressive Behaviors

When toddlers are stressed, they often revert back to old behaviors they had recently given up. For example, a toddler who is perfectly able to walk may suddenly begin crawling again or want to be held by Mom or Dad all the time. Other regressive behaviors include thumb sucking, sleeping in the parent's bed, and wetting his or her pants. These behaviors often signal a reversion to comforting things when life is full of changes or stress.

During a divorce, parents often complain about their children's regressive behavior, but they should not make a big deal out of it. In fact, it's best to give the behavior minimal attention. These behaviors are normal and usually do not last very long. The following is the story of a client, "Barry," whom I saw for therapy after he became overwhelmed with one of his daughter's regressive behaviors after his divorce.

Barry was a twice-divorced dad to three young daughters. Additionally, he was living with his girlfriend, "Lydia," who had a six-year-old daughter. Every other weekend, Barry's three daughters and Lydia's daughter were all at the house together—four girls under the age of seven. Barry's youngest daughter, "Juliet," was very unhappy about having to share her dad's attention. Although Juliet was four and a half and had been sleeping in her own big-girl bed for over a year, when she was at Barry's house she would creep into Barry and Lydia's room and snuggle up in their bed.

Lydia became uncomfortable with Juliet in their bed, especially because she thought Barry's two ex-wives would completely "freak out" if they knew about it. Barry tried to talk to Juliet about the situation, to no avail. Juliet would tear up and say that she was lonely and missed Daddy when she was alone at night. Barry kept giving in and allowing Juliet into the bed, which began to cause serious problems between Barry and Lydia.

When I met with Barry and Lydia, Barry said his biggest concern was that Juliet always had been able to snuggle when he was married to her mother and he didn't want to make Juliet think there was anything wrong with her wanting to climb into his bed. After processing the pros and cons of the situation and both Barry's and Lydia's feelings, we decided on a plan that would get Juliet out of Barry's bed without hurting her feelings while still allowing her special closeness with her dad.

Barry went home and explained to all four girls that he had been thinking a lot about the sleeping arrangements and had come to a conclusion: "I was thinking that what if one night all four of you were scared or had a bad dream or something and you all wanted to come into our bed to snuggle? Well, there isn't room for four kids and two grown-ups in that bed, for sure, so I'd be forced to choose which kid got to stay and which ones had to go back to their own beds. That wouldn't be very fair at all, and I don't know how I could ever make that decision, so . . . I decided that no one can come into Daddy's bed in the middle of the night to snuggle, but any one of you girls can call me into your bed to snuggle with you. How does that sound?"

The girls seemed reluctant but agreed to Barry's plan. For the next two weeks, Barry reported he was exhausted because the girls began to try out the plan and they called him into their rooms repeatedly every night. For a while he thought the plan was not going to work, but shortly after the two-week period of "testing" was up, the novelty wore off and the girls went back to their normal sleeping schedules. The last week I saw Barry, he reported that Juliet had called him in only twice during the past week.

Storytelling

Toddlers are not always accurate storytellers. In fact, toddlers are very good at finding a grain of truth and creating a far more elaborate tale to tell about it. For this reason, when parents divorce, they must be careful not to automatically believe everything their children say, especially regarding things about the other parent. *Always confirm with the other parent any troublesome stories you may hear from your young child before accusing the other parent or getting angry.*

The good news about a toddler's love of storytelling and other games of make-believe is that they make it easier to talk about the divorce than you might think. For example, the court referred a two-and-a-half-year-old child, "Chase," to me for three therapy sessions to address the child's acting out during his parents' volatile divorce. Apparently Chase had been kicking and biting at preschool and had become very aggressive toward his father. I was initially uncertain of how much I would be able to get from such a young child in three sessions, but figured I'd give it a shot. The following is an overview of our first session together.

"Hi, Chase. My name is Lisa. I thought maybe we could play with these blocks together today. Do you like playing with blocks?" Chase nodded yes and went over to the laundry basket filled with heavy wooden blocks. We began to build up some sort of an edifice and soon I realized it looked a lot like a castle. I made a moat around the outside of the castle and explained to Chase what a moat was. I asked him if he'd rather have it filled with sharks or alligators. "Sharks," he replied.

Then I began finding items around the room to represent all his family members—Mom, Dad, Grandma; his babysitter; the preschool teacher. I started by putting a black ballpoint pen ("Dad") on top of the castle. Before I could even let go, Chase smacked the "Dad" off of the castle and across the room. I tried to place a pink eraser ("Mom") on top of the castle and again Chase hit her off. "Who is allowed on top of the castle, Chase?" Chase grabbed a small plastic gorilla that represented himself and placed it on top of the castle.

We went on with this play for at least twenty-five minutes and I was able to learn a lot about Chase's perspective without asking a single direct question about the divorce. I learned that Mommy always sat on the moat wall waiting to fall in. When she did fall in, it was Daddy who pushed her. When I asked him, "Who will save Mommy and pull her out of the moat?" Chase readily replied, "Me."

I was quickly able to understand that Chase had been pulled into his parents' arguments and his perception was that Daddy was hurting Mommy and that he felt he had to save her. My recommendation was further play therapy sessions with Chase, and I met with the parents for one session to discuss how I thought they could help Chase stay out of the middle.

If you are wondering how your toddler is feeling about your divorce and the changes it has brought, you might get more information from *not* asking directly about what you want to know. Playing with your child—making up stories, playing with dolls, and drawing pictures—can give you great insight into how your child sees the world and all that is going on around him or her.

THE DEVELOPMENTAL FEATURES OF THE PRESCHOOLER PHASE

This section highlights some of the main challenges that preschool children encounter and examines how divorce may affect this stage of development. This section also offers practical advice to divorcing parents on how to work together to help support preschool children at this difficult time of family changes.

Fantasy

Preschoolers are wonderful at fantasy play. This is the stage when they excitedly believe in the Easter Bunny and the Tooth Fairy and are certain they heard Santa's sleigh bells on the roof last Christmas Eve. Preschoolers hold their breath when they reach into the cereal box to pull out the game piece that promises "One in 5 billion will win a trip to Disney World," truly believing they have the winning one.

The problem with fantasy during a divorce is that children this age may spend a great deal of time believing Mom and Dad will get back together. Sometimes a preschooler will simply believe that if he or she is "good," then Mom and Dad will reunite. Preschoolers overestimate their own power and may fantasize about ways they can manipulate their parents back together. A conversation I once had with "Damien," a five-year-old boy I saw for therapy, makes an excellent example of the power of a preschooler's fantasy.

"Hi, Damien. How are things going in your family?" Damien smiled and said, "Well, my parents probably aren't getting divorced anymore." I figured Damien's parents probably would have updated me on their reconciliation if this had been the case, but I decided to ask, "Really? So what happened?"

Damien went on to describe how he told his mom that Dad had been asking about her. He also told Dad that Mom had been crying about missing him. Then he told Mom that Dad wasn't dating "Julie" anymore and that he really missed Mom a lot.

I asked Damien if his dad was really not seeing Julie anymore and he answered, "I don't know but now my mom thinks he's not and that's what's important."

Needless to say, I needed to bring Damien's parents into the next session to help Damien understand that they were not getting back together and that Damien simply didn't have the power to cause the divorce or stop it from happening.

If you are a divorcing parent of a preschooler, be aware that the child can misconstrue the slightest bit of cooperation between you and your ex-spouse as a sign you may be getting back together. There is a very fine line divorcing parents need to walk between working closely together for the sake of the children and sending a message of possible reconciliation. Given that the majority of children wish for their parents to get back together, they may interpret any little sign of friendliness or compatibility between the parents as an indication of possible reunification of the family to its predivorce state.

It is very important for divorcing parents to cooperate and engage regularly on issues related to the children and co-parenting. However, it is also important for parents (especially those who get along well) to be clear that although they will be working together, they will no longer be a married unit. It may be helpful to remind children that the reason the parents are getting along so well is because of the new relationship they have formed, rather than because the parents are thinking about getting back together.

If there is any chance that the parents are in fact considering reconciliation, they must be very careful to keep any confusing boundaries between them out of sight of the children until some solid decision about the relationship has been made. For example, children should not know if one parent has slept over at the other parent's house in the same bed, nor should they see lingering hugs or kisses. This protects the children from the pain of yet another loss if they begin to hope for a reconciliation that does not end up occurring.

Empathy

As children enter preschool age, they feel more empathy for others than they did when they were younger. Preschoolers can more readily recognize when another child is left out of the fun at the park, and if prompted, they may invite that child to join in.

During a divorce, preschoolers often feel empathy toward one or both parents. This is especially the case when one parent frequently cries or is visibly upset in front of the child. Often, the child may side with the parent whom he or she deems to be more of the victim of the divorce. A child might also become very clingy and have difficulty separating from that parent.

Be very careful not to play on your child's empathy. For example, you might hug your child and say, "Mommy is so sad about what Daddy has done to our family. C'mon and give Mommy a big hug to help me feel better." This places unnecessary responsibility on the child to both help you feel better and feel sorry for you. Being the "favorite" parent may feel good, but behind the child choosing sides are some complicated and painful feelings.

Demanding

Preschoolers are notorious for being demanding and sometimes quite bossy toward friends, siblings, and parents. A child may become even more demanding during a divorce in an attempt to gain some control over a situation that he or she largely has no control over at all. Parents do not sit down with children and ask them whether they want the parents to divorce or whether the children want to sell the house. The divorce and all the other decisions that come along with it are generally not things in which children participate. Therefore, many preschoolers will attempt to exert control.

Try to be patient with your children if they are bossy and demanding. Try to explain how being demanding makes others feel. You can also help your children by giving them *some* things to control. For instance, perhaps your child can be involved in choosing a new apartment or a new pet for the new home. Maybe your child can pick out a new comforter set to go on the bed at the new place or choose the color to paint one of the new rooms.

Ability to Reason

Preschoolers' brains are growing rapidly and their ability to reason improves every month. Many preschoolers are familiar with the word *divorce* and understand what it means. But because their thinking abilities are more advanced than when they were younger, they tend to try to determine the cause of their parents' divorce and may take on a sense of guilt and self-blame. One example is the story of "Crystal," a five-year-old child I saw for therapy.

I had been seeing Crystal for several weeks after her parents ("Ted" and "Gail") decided to divorce. Ted and Gail told me that Crystal "took the news of the divorce really hard" and refused to talk to them about it.

Shortly after one of our sessions began, Crystal burst into tears. I asked her if she wanted to tell me what was wrong. She nodded and said, "It's all my fault. My parents are getting divorced because of me." When I told Crystal I didn't think that was true at all, she responded, "Oh yes it is. I heard them say it. My parents were fighting over my room not being clean. If only I had kept my room clean, they wouldn't be getting divorced."

I then took a few minutes to speak alone with Ted and Gail. Ted and Gail told me that they had indeed been fighting about Crystal's room. Ted said, "I'm always the one who has to be on top of her to clean up the room. All you ever do is complain to me about everything, Gail, yet you never ask her to clean or anything else. You just dump on me all the time. If you want Crystal to take a bath or clean her room, for God's sake, ask her yourself to do it instead of yelling at me about it." It was clear to me that Ted and Gail's argument wasn't really about Crystal's room at all but rather about the expectations they had of each other.

After Crystal returned to the session, with all of us present, Ted and Gail spent the rest of the session explaining to Crystal that what she overheard was indeed them fighting about her messy room but that it wasn't really what they were arguing about. Gail said,

> All five-year-old children have messy rooms sometimes, Crystal, and we aren't at all mad about that. Messy rooms are part of life and your room is not the reason Daddy and I are getting divorced. Your room is just one of the many things we disagree on who should handle, but it is not at all the reason we are divorcing.

Crystal is a good example of how a child can take a few overheard words and twist them into a self-blaming scenario in which he or she is at fault for the parents' divorce. If you are divorcing, be very careful what you say in front of your children. They understand far more than you may give them credit for.

Using children's books as tools to help a child understand divorce can be a great thing to try at this developmental stage of a child's life. Many parents seek out books written *specifically* about divorce. However, many have told me they struggle with a good deal of the existing children's books on divorce because they contain some information that is not pertinent to their specific family or situation. Why trouble the child with issues like step-parenting or moving away if these are not yet issues in a particular child's life?

When working with children of divorce, I prefer to use books that normalize certain themes rather than talk about the specifics of divorce. For example, there are several books in the *Mama Rex & T* series (by Rachel Vail and Steve Björkman) that are wonderful tools for helping children understand single parenting. The stories involve a mother dinosaur and her son, with no mention of divorce or even why there is no paternal involvement. Mama Rex is a working mother who is very patient and calm with T while struggling to care for him, do her work, and do household chores. The books normalize a one-parent-one-child setup in which the single parent manages everything. The book highlights T's need to be patient sometimes while Mama Rex completes work on the computer before she can play with him. I find that some of the best books for children going through a divorce are simply the ones that normalize *different types of families*.

The following is a list of some other helpful titles:

- *Arthur* books by Lillian Hoban. Arthur and Violet are brother and sister monkeys who are largely raised by a motherly babysitter.

- *Little Witch* books by Deborah Hautzig. Little witch is raised by a "group effort" including her mother, aunt, and older sisters.

- *Arthur* books by Marc Brown. One of the main characters, Buster, lives with his mother and rarely sees his father because he is a pilot and is often out of the country.

- *Don't Wake Up Mama!* by Eileen Christelow. A mom raises five little monkeys.

- *Guess How Much I Love You?* by Sam McBratney. There is no mention of a mother in this sweet tale of the love between Big Nutbrown Hare and Little Nutbrown Hare.

- *Little Bear* series by Else Holmelund Minarik and Maurice Sendak. One of the main characters, Emily, is raised by her grandmother.

- *A Day With Dad* by Bo R. Holmberg. A father lives in a different town but comes in on the train to spend a special father-son day together.

- *A Tale of Two Mommies* by Vanita Oelschlager. The story highlights the loving, caring nature of families that remains the same, regardless of the gender of the parents in the household.

- *And Tango Makes Three* by Justin Richardson and Peter Parnell. Two male penguins fall in love and raise a baby together.

The following books may also help you help your children talk about their feelings in general without pressuring them to talk about the divorce directly.

- *The Way I Feel Books* by Cornelia Maude Spelman. Simple text; short, clear statements; and colorful pictures dealing with such topics as "When I Feel Good About Myself."

- *Let's Talk About . . .* by Joy Wilt Berry. Kid-friendly descriptions and compelling tales of topics such as feeling angry, feeling sad, and needing attention.

- *It's Okay to Be Different* by Todd Parr. A silly, colorful book on being okay even when you're different.

- *How Are You Peeling?* by Saxton Freymann and Joost Elffers. A creative book that uses real carved fruits and vegetables to represent facial expressions that denote certain feelings like anger or joy.

- *Angry Octopus: A Relaxation Story* by Lori Lite. A wonderful tale, with strategies for young children to relax and breathe woven into the storyline.

- *The Way I Feel* by Janan Cain. Rhyming text that portrays children's emotions like frustration and jealousy.

- *Love You Forever* by Robert Munsch. The story of the depths of undying love a mother has for her child, no matter what happens.

- *I Was So Mad* by Mercer Mayer. A playful exploration of feelings.

- *The Giving Tree* by Shel Silverstein. This classic story covers a range of feelings, from joy to feeling abandoned, with two beloved characters (a boy who turns into a man and a tree) and the changing nature of their relationship over time.

Imitation

Preschool children frequently imitate others. This is how they learn about the different roles people have in families and in the world. Preschoolers often design games where one child will play "the mommy" and another might play "the big brother." It is common to hear a child speaking in different tones and using particular verbiage when pretending to be someone else.

Preschoolers can be particularly prone to acting like "mini" mommies and daddies in the household; a child may know that mom always says, "No snacks before dinner—we're almost ready to eat," and so the child may go around acting like Mom, telling younger siblings to "get out of the pantry because it's almost dinnertime."

Because young children regularly engage in such imitation of others and role-playing, it is no wonder that during a divorce a preschooler might try to fill the role of whichever parent is absent on a given day. This can be terribly annoying to the other siblings in the house. Try to be patient with the youngster who is "playing parent," but also be sure to let the child know that although you appreciate the help, he or she is not responsible for policing the household. Encourage the child to go play outside or help set the table to avoid parentifying the child.

On another note, because preschool children imitate others, particularly their parents, it is extremely important that during a divorce parents behave in an appropriate manner. Children watch and learn from their parents and will frequently treat others in the family as the parent does. The child will express anger in the way he or she sees the parents express it. If Mom throws objects at Dad when they are fighting, the child may then start throwing things when he or she is angry. Likewise, if a child overhears Dad calling Mom "weak" and a "no-good liar," the child may begin calling Mom these names, too. *As difficult as it may be during the trying times of divorce, you must set a positive example for your impressionable young children and refrain from poor behavior.*

8

SPECIAL ISSUES FOR
SCHOOL-AGE CHILDREN

Nothing you do for children is ever wasted.
—GARRISON KEILLOR (American author and storyteller)

Every effort is worth your while when trying to adhere to best-practice parenting during a divorce. One day, many years from now, your child will be acutely aware of how you handled your divorce. I have had adult children of divorce come up to me in every parenting class and tell me how grateful they are for certain things they remember a parent doing to help ease the pain of that divorce. One woman said, "The one thing I remember is that my mother *never* talked bad about my father. I was allowed to think he was the best and even put him on a pedestal, and she never told me otherwise. I figured out in my own time who my father really was and that he was unreliable and controlling, but my mother never forced me to have to see that back then."

Major changes in the family, such as divorce, can be very hard on school-age kids. This chapter focuses on the developmental features of children at this stage and explores some ways in which a divorce can interrupt the normal milestones that occur during this time frame. I also make suggestions as to how to handle tricky situations divorce can create.

THE DEVELOPMENTAL FEATURES OF THE SCHOOL-AGE PHASE

There are a number of developmental features that are common in children between the ages of seven and eleven. A divorce at this tender stage may interfere with a child's normal psychological and emotional growth.

Expanded Number of Attachment Figures

When a child enters the school-age years, the number of adults he or she comes in contact with increases greatly. There may now be teachers, other children's parents, coaches, and instructors for such things as religious education or dance or art classes who engage regularly with a child. The child will form different emotional bonds with each of these people and learn a variety of things from them. The relationships that the child forms with these people may make them attachment figures (see chapter 7 for more information on attachment figures).

During a divorce, these other adults in your child's life can offer emotional support to your child. Consider informing these important people about your divorce. Some children will refrain from telling other people because they are embarrassed about it or simply don't want to talk about it. But if there are other healthy, adult attachment figures in your child's life, they can help the child talk about the situation and what he or she might be feeling. These other adults may also be able to offer your child advice and suggestions as to how to cope when you and your former spouse are fighting or when he or she is worried about one of you. A good example of this is the following excerpt from a session I had with a nine-year-old boy, "Mickey," whose parents were going through an unfriendly divorce.

"So, Mickey, how's everything with you?" I asked.

"Not so good," he answered. "My parents are fighting even more now. Every night it's the same thing. My mom accuses my dad of drinking too much and that always starts a big argument. They yell and scream and swear for hours. I usually can't even fall asleep until after midnight because they are so loud. I hate it. I hate being at home. I hate them."

"Wow," I responded. "That sounds really tough, Mick."

Mickey nodded and said, "The only thing that helps a little bit is something my school social worker told me. My parents signed me up for some lame divorce group for kids at lunchtime two days a week at school. It's stupid but I like the social worker who does the group. Her name is Sam. I think it's short for Samantha actually." Mickey stopped speaking.

After a few moments I said, "So what did Sam tell you to do to make it better when your parents are fighting?"

"Well, she said two things actually. First, she said I had the right to go downstairs and ask them to please stop fighting. And she said I should try listening to music or writing things down or imagining I'm somewhere else. So I think about being at an amusement park. Riding on roller coasters and eating cotton candy and going on the water slides."

"Sounds like Sam had some good ideas for you. So you've tried doing all these things?" I asked.

"Well, I haven't asked them to stop fighting because I try not to get involved, but I do draw sometimes or put on my iPod. But mostly thinking about the rides works the best."

Mickey's parents were so caught up in their own unhappiness that they were unable to stop their fighting, let alone work with Mickey on some coping tools to help him get through this tough time. Although immediate family members may no longer be the only role models in the child's life, this isn't necessarily a bad thing when a family is experiencing a divorce. These other attachment figures can help bolster your child against the negative effects a divorce, especially a volatile one, can bring.

Pride in Accomplishments

School-age children typically become proud of their accomplishments and want their parents to hear about what they've done: "Look at what I made in art class today, Mom!"; "Guess what, Dad? I got the lead part in my school play"; and "Listen to the poem I wrote for Earth Day."

For school-age children especially, the absence of a parent after divorce is a big loss. It's one less person around to share in the child's joy of making a sports team at school, one less parent around to help out with math homework. Divorcing parents should try to encourage the child to share good news and accomplishments with *both* parents, regardless of whether they are in the home at the time. For example, if a child comes home excited and babbling to Mom about a special award he received at school for neatness and organization, Mom should encourage the child to let Dad in on the news, too. She could say something like, "Wow! That's great news! All your extra effort really paid off. Why don't you give Dad a quick call and let him know you won this award? I'm sure he'd be really proud and maybe he can help you think of a good spot to hang the award in your room."

Sometimes children will not rush to one parent to share news for fear of hurting the other parent's feelings. By encouraging your child to share important news with your ex-spouse, you send an unspoken message that it is okay to love the other parent, and in doing so, you remove your child from that impossible decision-making spot.

A simple, practical way for both you and your former spouse to celebrate your child's accomplishments and show your interest in the child's work is to display good grades or your child's artwork in *each* of your homes. Doing this will also help the child feel at home in both places.

Concrete Thinking

Although abstract-thinking abilities are just beginning to bud in older school-age children, many younger school-age children are mostly concrete thinkers. In other words, they tend to see things in black-and-white terms. For example, a young child will see Mom and Dad fighting and assume that because Dad is yelling, he must be the one who is at fault because he is being mean to Mom. Young children cannot look at outside, influential factors and the underlying factors that may have some bearing on any given situation.

Given this penchant for concrete thought, it follows that children at this age are also not able to understand the need for complex solutions to problems. The following monologue by an eleven-year-old girl, "Kylie," whom I saw for therapy during her parents' difficult divorce, is a good example.

> My parents are so stupid. They fight over the dumbest things. And they tell *me* I pick on my brother about every little thing. I don't get why they don't see it—all Mom has to do is *shut up* for once. She has to start on my father the second he gets home from work: "Take off your shoes, they're muddy. Why wasn't this bill paid that I got a late notice for in the mail today? Oh, sure, go sit down and read the paper and relax while I make dinner and help the kids with homework."

> God, she just never stops, my mother . . . and so my dad
> gets all pissed off and storms upstairs and no one sees him again
> for the night. And then my mom really does have to do it all by
> herself but she asked for it by starting up with my dad.

Although Kylie's explanation seems brilliant in its simplicity on one level, there is often much more underlying parents' fights than a pair of muddy shoes or an unpaid bill. Kylie is a good example of concrete thinking: straightforward, simple, limited.

Remember, too, that parents are partially to blame for their children's lack of understanding about fighting and divorce. Parents never allow their children to end a relationship with another family member when things get difficult or arguments occur. For instance, let's say two siblings are fighting in the back of the car one day, and one yells to Mom, "Stop! Pull over! Johnny's hitting me and keeps pushing onto my side of the seat. Make him get out of the car, Mom . . . I don't want him as a brother anymore." Does the mother then pull over and dump Johnny out of the car and say, "Sorry, Johnny, but you pick on your sister too much so you're out of the family now. Good-bye."? Of course not! The mother will probably say something like, "Stop the fighting, kids. Each of you stay on your own side of the seat and keep your hands to yourself."

Parents typically give their children tools to fix things or to get through an argument. Parents preach things like, "Say you're sorry" or "Take turns to be fair"; they do not say, "Okay, you don't need to speak to your mother again, because she yelled at you this morning. We'll make her move to the basement."

Due to parents' messages, most children have a hard time understanding how their parents are allowed to simply give up and dissolve their marital relationships. *Family members aren't just supposed to walk away from each other; family is forever.* As much as you'd like to, it is probably impossible to convince your child that divorce is a good option. It is better to focus on *showing* your child a healthier, more peaceful life after divorce.

More Judgmental and Critical of Self and Others

As children enter the school-age years, they often become increasingly judgmental of themselves and others. They are quick to say, "I hate this teacher—she's so unfair," or, "I don't like Sarah—she's too bossy and thinks she's so cool."

For this reason, school-age children are also very quick to judge one or both parents when a divorce happens in the family. A child will look for an easy explanation as to who's at fault for the breakup so it is easier to know whom to be angry at. Children are often wrong in their assumptions of who's at fault, however. As discussed, concrete thinking often causes children to come to overly simplistic conclusions that do not take into account the levels of complexity that exist in many marital relationships and divorces.

If your child is treating you as the "at-fault" parent, take comfort that this sort of judgment is developmentally normal for school-age children. The best way to convince a child that you are not the awful person he or she may want to believe you are is to show it in the way you relate to the child. For example, if a child blames you for the divorce and says it's because you are "always yelling at everyone," perhaps you could focus on *not* yelling at anyone while the child is around. If a child experiences a behavior from one parent *other* than the behavior (yelling) being pegged as the cause of the divorce, it will challenge the child's perception and possibly lead to a paradigm shift that will help the child forgive the parent.

It's also important to remember that if your child asks you a direct and inappropriate question (e.g., "Have you been cheating on Mom and that's why she's divorcing you?"), it is often not because your child wants to hear the truthful answer, but rather to find a solid reason to help him or her know whom to blame and be angry at. Remember to answer these sorts of questions accordingly; never give too much information just because a child asks for it. Think about what your child is asking for. In the case of the aforementioned question of "cheating," the child does not want to hear Dad respond with the sordid details of his affair with a coworker. Rather, the child is looking for something to peg on Dad that makes the divorce make sense. The child is looking for a simple, concrete understanding: *If Dad cheated on Mom, then he is a jerk and I hate him because he's the reason Mom's divorcing him and we have to move and our whole family is changing.*

School-age children can also be quite critical of themselves. This is why it is very important to tell your child *often* that the divorce is not his or her fault. However, this is often not enough. You need to be careful as well about the nonverbal messages you send during this very difficult time of sadness and change. If you become overwhelmed and exasperated, you may respond to your children in a way that suggests blame for the divorce. For instance, if you are emotional and overtired, you may say, "What is it? What do you want from me now?" in response to a child's question. The message the child receives may be that he or she asks too much of you, which then may be further twisted in the child's mind to mean, "I am the reason you are so tired and crabby all the time and the reason Mom [or Dad] left." Of course, we all know this is not the case, but during a child's stage of easy self-criticism, it is important to be careful about what you say and how you say it.

Another common venting theme for overwhelmed parents is, "Why do you have to be so lazy and not do anything around the house? All you do is walk around making messes and destroying things. You can't even keep your own room halfway decent—it's a total pigsty." Words are powerful tools; be especially careful of how you use them with school-age children.

Increased Self-Reliance

School-age children become increasingly more self-reliant with each passing year. They may begin to snub their parents' offers to help them with tasks and reject their parents' attempts to talk with them about sensitive issues like dating and drugs. When a divorce occurs during this stage of development, some parents find it worrisome that the child turns down their help and comfort. It is normal for these children to say things such as "It's no big deal" or "I'm fine" in response to their parents' questions of how they're doing or feeling about something. Yet when dealing with a divorce in the family, no child can really handle it all on his or her own, regardless of how self-reliant the child may think he or she is.

The good part about self-reliance in school-age children is that there are many things around to support and distract them; children engage with friends and are involved in sports, school, other activities—even favorite TV shows—that are separate from family. A school-age child can seek out avenues to escape the pain of family troubles in other things and with other people. However, not all these things or people may be healthy outlets, so you should be monitoring what things your child is doing and with whom. The following is a good example of good versus bad self-reliant avenues that a child can take when dealing with a divorce at home.

"Thad" (age eleven) and his mom, "Roxanne," came to therapy to discuss Roxanne's concerns over how Thad was dealing with his parents' split. Roxanne and her husband, "Thaddeus," were in the middle of a very bitter divorce. There had been a great deal of fighting in the household and Roxanne had finally borrowed enough money from her sister to be able to move Thad and herself out of the house and into a small condominium nearby. Although the fighting had decreased significantly since the move, Roxanne was concerned that Thad wasn't really talking to her about how he was feeling, had begun to spend a lot of time on the computer, and was acting "kinda depressed."

I met with Roxanne and Thad a couple of times (Thaddeus refused to come to a session) before asking to meet with Thad alone. He told me that when his parents were fighting, he'd just leave the house and go hang out at one of his friends' houses in the neighborhood. Now that they had moved, Thad had no escape, because he didn't know anyone in the condo. Because he had been used to playing with friends, he had been able to avoid thinking about the divorce. Now he described himself as feeling very lonely and having a lot of time to think about the divorce (hence the depressed mood Roxanne had noted).

Thad told me that he had begun e-mailing with a girl, "Mia," he met at camp the previous summer and that she was helping him because her parents got divorced two years earlier. The problem with this online friendship, I soon discovered, was that Mia was "preparing" Thad for what to expect by telling him the horror stories of her own parents' divorce. Mia's advice to Thad was frequently wrong; in one e-mail she had written, "Just start pulling away from your dad now. It will make it easier when you start to barely ever see him at all. Now that you've moved out and you're with your mom, she'll start really keeping him away from you." In anticipation of all the bad stuff to come, Thad found himself in a growing state of loneliness and depression.

Thad's original involvement with and escape to his friends in the neighborhood were good buffers for him against the troubles at home. But the loss of these friends in the move, coupled with the narrow and negative perspective he was receiving from Mia, made for a very depressing combination for him.

Although self-reliance can be a good thing for children of divorce, you need to be careful to remember that your child still needs parental support, involvement, and monitoring. *Support your child's healthy "escapes" and watch out for those that may send up unhealthy warning flags.*

Increased Egocentrism

School-age children become increasingly egocentric with each passing year. They most often focus on how any given situation will particularly affect their own lives and well-being. For instance, children in this age category will often make the choice of whom to support in a presidential race based on one or two simple issues ("I want John XYZ to be president because he won't make us pay more taxes and won't go to war"). This kind of concrete thinking is the impetus for belief in the simple notion that war is wrong, and the developmental self-focus is responsible for the narrow-minded thought that people shouldn't give hard-earned money to the government when they could be using it for a vacation or a new pool.

Likewise, when a divorce happens in the family, a child may view many components of the event through a very self-focused lens. Knowing this can help divorcing parents answer children's questions. When a child asks something like, "Are we going to have to move?" the child is really asking, "Will I have to leave my neighborhood and friends? Will I have to go to a new school?" *When children ask you questions, try to answer them with information that satiates their need to know how things will directly affect them.*

Because school-age children frequently view life as it directly affects them, it is also common for children of divorce in particular to think that the whole world is watching them. These children may think that everybody will know about the divorce and "think we're crazy." If a related domestic incident or DUI is listed in the paper, children may suffer great embarrassment and fear that the entire town will know about it and judge them by it. Any public fighting between the divorcing parents may elicit a similar response from children.

Try to keep your disagreements away from the public eye to spare your child the discomfort of others being involved in your family business. Also, be careful not to reaffirm this embarrassment through your own actions; don't be afraid to say, "You know what? Everybody has his or her own set of problems and this just happens to be our family's tough time. People who treat us differently or judge us because of this just haven't been in our shoes. We can't blame them for what they don't know, but you'll find out that there are lots of people who will understand and be very supportive of us. There's nothing to be embarrassed about."

The following is the story of a mom, "Hope," and her two children, "Noelle" and "Drew," and how the children's self-focus led to a great deal of anxiety and stress for them.

> Hope and her two children, Noelle (age 12) and Drew (age 8), came in for therapy with me shortly after Hope filed for divorce from her abusive husband, "Dennis." Hope and the children had moved in with Hope's mother while they waited for their house to sell so they would have money to buy a condo. Hope complained that the children had both become very withdrawn and angry with her, and she was concerned about their behavior.
>
> After meeting alone with each of the children for several sessions each, I was able to ascertain that both Noelle and Drew had their own reasons for being depressed and angry. First, unbeknownst to Hope, Noelle's best friend had begun to distance herself from Noelle and rumor had it that this friend's parents wouldn't allow the friend to visit Noelle at her grandmother's house because it was in a bad part of town. Noelle had also heard several kids talking behind her back about how they read in the paper that her father had been arrested for being "a drunk and a wife beater." One kid actually said to Noelle, "You're already starting to turn into white trash." Noelle disclosed to me that she hated her mother for stirring everything up by calling the cop, filing for divorce, and making Noelle's life miserable.
>
> Drew, on the other hand, had been very sad about losing regular contact with his friends in the old neighborhood and was very concerned that their two large Saint Bernards wouldn't be able to go with them when they left grandma's house.
>
> I brought the family back into a session together and, with the kids' permission, explained to Hope some of the reasons the kids were angry. I worked with the kids to help them understand how they were displacing their anger on Mom.

Noelle provides an excellent example of a school-age child's embarrassment and self-focused views. She also demonstrates concrete thinking ("Mom's at fault for having to go and stir everything up") and the inability to look at the bigger picture (Mom needed to save the family from a dangerous, abusive situation).

Try to be patient and understanding with your school-age children's simple thinking and erroneous conclusions. Keep the children's mind-set in mind to help you understand the motivation for some of their anger and other negative feelings or fears. Try to keep an avenue of communication open with your children so they can feel comfortable venting these frustrations to you.

Fear of Abandonment

Many school-age children worry that perhaps one parent might get mad at the child and "divorce" him or her at some point as well. Parents need to tell their school-age children frequently that they will not ever "divorce" the children no matter what they might do or say. *Parents are forever.*

School-age children often do not understand the common reasons their parents give them for the divorce—"We're just better off as friends"; "We fell out of love"; "We have different paths for the future"; "We don't agree on big, important things." Many children of divorce continue to believe that a parent may "fall out of love" with them if they are "bad," even if the parents regularly preach that this will not happen.

I commonly use several pieces of fruit to explain the difference between love of a spouse and love of a child to younger school-age children. The following is an example from a therapy session I had with a seven-year-old child, "LaKeesha," whose parents had recently divorced. LaKeesha's parents brought her in because they were very concerned about her "hypersensitivity" (bursting into tears) when one of her parents reprimanded her about something minor (like talking too loud or interrupting a parent on the phone). The parents reported being unsuccessful in getting LaKeesha to understand that neither parent would ever stop loving her.

I held out an oversize brown paper lunch bag to LaKeesha and asked, "Do you want to guess what I have in here?" LaKeesha shrugged but leaned forward to try to peek inside. I invited her to sit on the floor with me and I proceeded to spread out several pieces of fruit I had in the bag—one banana, one large orange, a smaller tangerine, a kiwi, and a grape.

"Okay, LaKeesha, let's figure out your family here." I told her the banana would represent her dad because he was the tallest and the orange would be her mom because she was the next biggest fruit and then I let LaKeesha pick whether the tangerine, the kiwi, or the grape should represent her. LaKeesha chose to be the kiwi because it was "brown and fuzzy." We laughed.

I explained that when two grown-ups choose to get married, they decide to try to fit together two very different people into one life. We listed all the differences between LaKeesha's mom and dad and also between the banana and the orange. "It's very hard to make these two very different lives fit together," I said. I poked the pointed tip end of the banana against the roundness of the orange—not a good fit! "But sometimes," I said as I rolled the orange into the "C-shaped" niche of the banana, "there's a way that the two very different people can make it fit. This is how two different people decide to fit together to share one life together in marriage."

Then I explained how when a child is born (in this case, the kiwi), it is able to always roll right around the mother and father, always touching, even though it is different in some ways from each of them. "This is how the love for a child works. It isn't a decision to join two lives, but rather something that happens naturally and is born into both parents' lives and can never be erased."

Parents don't necessarily need to use fruit to explain the love for a child and how it differs from the commitment to a marriage, but the tangible example of family love and relationships is often clearer for younger children.

Although school-age children begin to expand their attachments and relationships outside of the family, the family is still the secure base for children. I liken the relationship of a child with the family to the relationship between a child and a trampoline. The child must be grounded by the firm but pliable base of the trampoline in order to float and flip and fly. After some time "flying," the child must return to the secure base of the trampoline in order to get the support to take off again. This happens over and over again. Similarly, in order for the school-age child to go out into the world, the child must intermittently return to the secure home-base for the support he or she will need to take off again.

The family acts as a trampoline to the child, and the foundation of it must be strong and healthy. A divorce doesn't have to take away this strong but flexible base for the child; however, the stress and issues that sometimes occur in a divorce can detract from the strength of the family core. I ask parents in my divorce-parenting class to take a moment to think about the "feel" of their home lives. Are they rushed, disorganized, and full of yelling? Or are they calm, patient, and supportive? After the divorce, each parent will be separately responsible for making sure the "trampoline" at home is securely grounded and not full of dangerous holes. *Take the time to improve the child's home life if there are places to improve.* Your efforts in reinforcing your children's home-base will go far in terms of their happiness and well-being.

WHEN TO WORRY

So far I have highlighted the normal developmental features of the school-age years, examined how divorce can interfere with these stages, and offered suggestions for approaching specific issues that may arise. However, one of the biggest concerns divorcing parents have is knowing when a child's reaction is serious enough to warrant outside help. The following is an overview of some of the more serious signs parents should look for in their children when any traumatic event or big change occurs in the family. I also offer advice about when to worry.

When the Child Withdraws from Previously Enjoyed Activities or Friends

Some depression is normal for any child going through a drastic change (like a divorce) in the family. However, young children are not immune to serious depression. If your child withdraws from friends or activities, seems to be uninterested in everything, is sleeping more, or appears very sad for more than a week or so, it's wise to seek a professional consultation with a therapist. A school guidance counselor or social worker can meet with the child first and will probably be able to help with a referral to a therapist who is skilled and experienced in working with children.

When the Child Becomes a Miniparent Toward a Parent or Siblings

During or after a divorce, a school-age child may feel the need to step into the role of a miniparent. I find this to be especially true of the same-sex parent; perhaps Dad moves out and a ten-year-old son proceeds to take over his chores around the house and talks with Mom about how to discipline and handle the other children. Be very careful about not contributing to the miniparent scenario by dumping many of the absent parent's tasks on your child or by saying things like, "You're the oldest so you're going to be your brothers' role model now that Dad is not living here." *Being a miniparent takes away from the child's ability to experience childhood, resulting in many children growing up resentful of having been drawn into that role.*

When the Child Begins to Hit Himself or Herself
Some children express anger or sadness by taking it out on themselves. They bang their heads on the wall or pinch themselves when they get frustrated. Children can be prone to self-blame and become physically hurtful to themselves, especially during such a fragile time as a divorce in the family.

Sometimes children will beat up on themselves verbally as well. "I'm so stupid," "I hate myself," and "I want to kill myself" are common statements from distressed children. Whether physical or verbal, this sort of self-deprecating behavior warrants professional help to help your child develop better coping skills to deal with anger and sadness.

When the Child Experiences a Significant Drop in Grades
Some children deal with a divorce by throwing themselves full throttle into their schoolwork in an attempt to please and make things easier for their parents. But for other children, the sadness the divorce brings into the family can cause a child to become distracted or despondent at school, resulting in dropping grades. Although a drop in grades is common among children going through divorce, parents need to monitor the situation closely. A temporary decline may be enough to set a child behind for semesters to come, depending on what subject matter the child missed. Bad grades, if unusual for a child, may hurt his or her feelings of self-worth and cause a great deal of stress and extra "catching up" work for the child. *Calmly jump on a drop in grades right away and get your child the extra help he or she needs to get back on track with his or her homework and studies before the drop in grades turns into a bigger issue.*

When the Child Acts Out Behaviorally
A behavior problem at school can signal distress in a child, and you should look into it right away. Sometimes a child who acts out negatively at school may be asking for attention. During a difficult time like divorce, many parents find themselves distracted and unable to give enough time and attention to their children at home. Yet other children act out as an

attempt to draw their parents back together. Most parents, even those who are the least friendly with each other, will come together (at least temporarily) out of concern for a child with a problem.

Talk to the school counselor or social worker first to see what he or she recommends. Some schools offer "divorce groups" at school that can bring your child together with kids in similar circumstances and offer ways to deal with the feelings and events the family changes may bring forth.

Remember that some pain and adjustment is required of *all* children who experience divorce. Although many of the emotions and behaviors children exhibit during this difficult time are normal and expected, you know your children best. Help them by watching carefully for particular signs that may signal something more serious.

QUESTIONS DIVORCING PARENTS SHOULD DISCUSS

This book stresses the importance of ongoing, healthy communication between parents during and after a divorce as an important part of a child's adjustment to the family changes. The following is a list of key topics for divorcing parents to consider and discuss in order to work collaboratively in raising a child together, yet separately.

Will one (or both) parent(s) be responsible for talking to the child about important topics such as sex or drug and alcohol use?

If parents do not discuss important topics such as these or are not clear with each other about who will address these issues with the child, it may end up that no one does it at all! Additionally, if one parent has already brought up the "sex talk" with the child, for example, the other parent may have to have a talk about sex sooner than he or she expected.

What is an appropriate age for the child to be left alone?

This is a very important topic for divorcing parents to discuss. It has been the source of many fights between parents in my therapy room. If one parent leaves the child home alone and the other parent is not comfortable with the arrangement, the uncomfortable parent should at least have the opportunity to talk to the child about safety concerns or encourage him or her to call and check in. The age at which a parent should leave one child alone and in charge of younger siblings is an essential area of discussion as well. Factors such as the maturity level of the child, how difficult younger siblings might be to manage, and how comfortable the child is alone are important considerations.

What is an acceptable age for dating?

Dating may or may not become an issue during these school-age years for your child, but it is a good topic for divorcing parents to explore. If a child is allowed to date, what will this entail? Will the parent chaperone the child and his or her date to the movies, or will the parent just drop the kids off and pick them up later? Coming to an agreement on this subject will help parents plan on what to discuss with their child regarding issues such as safety and how to get help if he or she is uncomfortable and there is no parent around.

What are the rules at each parent's home regarding television and computer usage?

Certain discussions with children will become more important and more pressing if one parent is allowing a child to have a great deal of unsupervised television and/or computer time. The child may be exposed to certain content or advanced knowledge that the other parent may not expect the child to come into contact with yet. Therefore, the parent will have to talk to the child accordingly.

Will the parents agree to have consequences in both households for poor behavior?

Although it is not imperative that *both* parents enforce similar repercussions at each of their homes for a serious misdeed by a child, doing so sends a stronger, more unified message. In any case, knowing whether both parents will support a consequence is good knowledge to have so that each parent can keep the child from manipulating the situation.

Are parents willing to discuss and decide on who gets what birthday or other holiday gift for a child before purchasing it?

I have seen so many divorcing families in which one parent goes out and buys a special gift (like the child's first cell phone or a newly released video game) without consulting the other parent, thereby cornering the market on the coolest gifts. Not only does this steal the thunder from the other parent, but it is just plain silly for parents not to compare notes with each other regarding what a child may or may not already have. It is better to take turns buying a specially desired gift for a child or for both parents to buy a particular gift for the child together.

What is the normal bedtime at each home?
This is very important information for parents to exchange with each other. Knowing what the bedtime is in each household explains a great deal about the mood a child may be in when he or she arrives at the other parent's home. If a parent believes the child is not getting enough sleep at the other parent's home, he or she can plan to make up that lost time when the child is with him or her. Lack of sleep can be a simple explanation for irritable or moody behavior and may rule out something more serious going on with the child.

What constitutes a "good enough" reason for a child to miss parenting time with one parent?
Many divorcing parents battle when one parent's schedule overlaps with the other parent's parenting time. The best practice is for each parent to *never* schedule on the other parent's time. However, as school-age children become more socially active and involved in sports and other hobbies, some scheduling flexibility is required. Divorcing parents should discuss plans that interfere with the other parent's time. Additionally, if a parent gives up his or her parenting time so that a child can attend some special event, both parents should arrange to make up for the missed visit if it is agreeable to both. This rescheduling sends the message to the child that the parent missed him or her.

How does the after-school ritual run at each home?
It is helpful to know what the after-school ritual looks like at the other parent's home. This can help a parent know what to expect in terms of homework and being prepared and packed up for the next day at school. This is especially true for midweek visits where the child will return for bedtime at the other parent's home. The parent will know when the child should have his or her homework done.

Also, all children need some downtime. Parents should talk with each other about how rushed and scheduled the child will be while in one parent's care so the other parent can work in some relaxation for the child when he or she returns home.

How does each parent feel about keeping secrets from the other parent?

If one parent readily keeps certain things from the other parent, it is nice to know about this little fact. Although it is not mandatory that parents exchange all information they have about a child, if one parent regularly withholds things, the other parent will have to be more careful in monitoring things such as the child's mood. If a child is being bullied at school or had an argument with a sibling that really upset him or her and one parent is unaware of these occurrences, that parent may wonder why the child is being oversensitive and irritable lately. Keeping a healthy, supportive, nonjudgmental line of communication open with your child is the best defense against being left out of big events in the child's life.

How will each parent bring up the idea of dating and introducing a new partner to the child?

Divorcing parents should discuss how they will approach the idea of dating and a new partner with the children. Will the parent introduce the new person as a "friend" or a "boyfriend" or "girlfriend"? Will the new partner sleep in the same room as the parent while the children are home? Will the parent encourage the children to call the new person by his or her first name? With younger children especially, will stepparents be called "Mommy" or "Daddy"? If parents discuss these sorts of questions ahead of time, it can save them both a great deal of stress and miscommunication. Additionally, when parents know something, whether good or bad, about their ex-spouse's parenting, they will know what to talk about—and how—with their children before any particular event occurs.

*   *   *

In closing, one of the most wonderful things about school-age children is their ability to recover quickly. Although not *all* children are resilient when there is a traumatic change (like a divorce) in the family, with some effort parents can play a huge part in buffering their children from the negative effects of divorce.

9

SPECIAL ISSUES FOR ADOLESCENTS

It's difficult to decide whether growing pains are something teenagers have—or are.
—AUTHOR UNKNOWN

Everyone knows that adolescents have notorious reputations. "Rebellious," "moody," "sarcastic," "lazy," and "emotional" are just a few of the labels teens frequently carry. Most parents are not surprised by the increasingly testy attitudes their children develop as they enter their adolescent years. Many parents *are* surprised, however, to learn that teenagers are one of the groups of children most seriously affected by the divorce process and its aftermath.

I have worked with many divorcing couples who have adolescent children. The majority I've seen express feelings of relief that their kids are out of their preteen years and "won't be as devastated by the divorce as they would be when they were little." Don't be sucked into this fallacy. *Adolescents frequently have difficulty adjusting to the split, especially if there are other stressors in play at the same time, such as bullying at school, peer pressure, breaking up with a boyfriend or girlfriend, drug use, behavioral problems, or undiagnosed mental health issues.* Remember that a vital part of your child's adjustment is the quality of your relationship during the divorce process (particularly the level of fighting or violence children witness), so it's best to keep things friendly.

Unfortunately, parents of adolescents are often less cautious about shielding their children from their fighting, and as a result teenagers are often much more aware of their parents' hostility toward each other than are younger children. In addition, as children grow older, their personal lives become more complicated. If parents divorce when their children are adolescents, it's likely the news may accompany any number of other pressures they may be experiencing, such as those mentioned.

It's important to remember that every adolescent is different, and the ways in which each reacts to the news of the divorce (and the subsequent reality of what changes it will bring) may vary greatly as well. A normal range of expected emotions includes angry outbursts, saddened mood, struggles for control, withdrawal from the family, and sometimes an uncharacteristic clinginess to one or both parents. At times, teens may not seem to be affected by the divorce at all—a situation that can be very distressing to the parents. This seemingly indifferent stance can be a completely normal reaction for some adolescents, many of whom will have a delayed response once family changes occur. Some adolescents adjust to divorce and family changes quite well and do not experience any problematic reactions. Generally speaking, though, teens who adjust best to a divorce do so when both parents are working hard to keep their children's best interests in mind.

THE DEVELOPMENTAL FEATURES OF ADOLESCENCE

Researchers and childhood-development specialists have found that during the stages of early, middle, and late adolescence teens typically have to conquer several challenges in order to grow emotionally and cognitively into young adults. It's especially important for parents going through a divorce to be aware of these developmental issues. Recognizing them helps parents to anticipate what reactions their teenagers might have to the changes taking place within their family. It also helps them to understand how their divorce may interrupt or affect how their child works through these normal developmental stages.

The Desire to Detach from Parents
The slow detachment from one's parents is a normal part of adolescence. At this point in time teens must begin to prepare to live on their own. A natural annoyance with one's parents often begins to develop,

along with an increased desire for space and privacy. Teenagers struggle with feeling caught between not wanting their parents around and still needing them desperately. When a divorce occurs during this time, teens can feel insecure due to the family's disruption. They may feel the natural desire to push their parents away but still worry about them and feel guilty about not being there for them.

Some teens will seem to remain just as detached from their parents as they were prior to the divorce and may stay away from the family as much as possible. But sometimes this distance is more about avoiding the fighting and family stress at home rather than a natural teenage-detachment drive. Other teens will go to the opposite extreme and cling to one parent while abandoning much of his or her social life. It's not developmentally natural, for instance, for a seventeen-year-old to stay home every weekend watching movies with a parent instead of going out with friends or talking on the phone with a new romantic interest.

It's important to watch for abrupt changes in behavior or signs of drug use in teens who spend a great deal of time away from you. Occasionally, teenagers whose parents are divorcing may try to blunt the pain of family problems by self-medicating with alcohol or drugs. Possible signs of drug or alcohol use include red or bloodshot eyes; a sloppy appearance; a lethargic or overly excited demeanor; the smell of alcohol or smoke on the breath, hair, or clothes; weight loss or gain; defiance; missing money or valuables; truancy; falling grades; memory problems; a change in friends; lying; disrespect; lateness in coming home; loss of interest in the family; increased time in the teen's room; and the appearance of matches, rolling papers, seeds, Baggies, pipes, or other possible drug paraphernalia.

The Increasing Importance of Peers

It's natural for teenagers to gravitate more and more toward their peers. During a divorce, teens' peers can be extremely helpful in cheering them up and helping them vent about frustrations at home. But not all teens confide in their friends. Over the years I've seen many adolescents who are embarrassed by their parents' divorce and, as a consequence, hide the breakup and its stress from their friends. One sixteen-year-old went so far as to tell his friends that his dad was staying at a grandmother's house indefinitely because she was very ill and needed his father to care for her. He told me he'd rather die than admit that his parents (whom all his friends liked and respected) were splitting up.

Parents should encourage teenagers to hang out with friends, and parents should have these friends over to the home frequently. This makes it easier to gauge their teens' social interaction with peers and helps their teenagers feel more comfortable and supported during difficult times at home. At the same time, you will be sending the message that you acknowledge your son's or daughter's need for social attachment.

The Need to Challenge Authority

Challenging authority and testing limits and boundaries set by others is a normal part of adolescent development. However, during a divorce parents sometimes wonder whether their teenagers' challenging behavior or defiance is due to adolescent development or a response to the changes taking place within the family. Sometimes teens will more readily test parental authority if they see their parents are not united and are showing signs of weakness. When parents are beaten down and at odds with each other, a teen may take advantage of the situation simply because he or she *can*.

There are ways you can deal with these situations. First, minimize the opportunities your teenager may have to manipulate the lack of unity between you and your ex-spouse. Stay as cohesive as possible on parenting and disciplinary issues by keeping your fighting far away from your teenager and by enforcing rules or curfews that were set prior to the divorce. Giving in too much can lead the teen to believe there is more room for noncompliance or breaking the rules.

Second, try to give your teenager choices whenever possible to let him or her know that you acknowledge the validity of his or her thoughts and beliefs—especially the teen's need to create and express an opinion.

If you're living apart from your teenager and planning a meeting, you can ask for input as to where you should meet and what you should do together. Likewise, you can insist that your teen treat a new boyfriend or girlfriend respectfully, even if you don't like the person. You might also give him or her the option of participating—or not—in some family activity or outing when the boyfriend or girlfriend will be there.

The Prevalence of Opinionated Thinking

Teenagers do a great deal of their thinking in concrete ways. They often adhere to strong political or ethical stances. They may become quite outspoken about the moral issue of the death penalty or stage a boycott against pesticide use in the school building. Or they may suddenly decide that they will not go to college. Although these common (but often short-term) decisions can disrupt family or school life and are a source of frustration for adults, they are nonetheless an integral part of an adolescent's growth.

Teens will often perceive concepts and situations in black-or-white terms. For example, a teen who recently became a devout vegetarian may believe that eating meat is wrong and may be unwilling to either hear or consider other points of view.

Likewise, during a divorce, teens may form powerful opinions in response to things they have witnessed. For instance, the heartache experienced in watching parents battle through the process of divorce can push teens to adopt strong views against relationships or marriage. As a result, they may break off relationships with girlfriends or boyfriends because they "don't want to be tied down." Teens may also extol the virtues of being single and swear that they will never get married so that they will never "need to depend on anyone."

Often, teenagers whose parents are divorcing will ally with one parent because they have decided that the other parent has committed some wrongful act. They may refuse to talk to one parent because they believe the parent's decisions were "unfair." It's often difficult to get teens to look at the more abstract, external forces that may have influenced parents' decisions.

In dealing with these situations, stick to simple explanations and don't feel compelled to defend yourselves or work overtime to convince your teen of the validity of your point of view. Take encouragement from the fact that soon your teenager will develop the ability to think more abstractly.

Understanding Self-Absorbed Behavior

Teens are well-known for their egocentric and self-absorbed ways. Normal adolescent development includes being overly concerned about one's physical appearance, abilities (or lack thereof), and perception by peers. Teenagers are frequently found peeking in mirrors, sizing up others, and agonizing over what to wear. Insecurities can nag them on a daily basis.

Be aware that this self-absorption is important to consider when speaking to your teenagers about your divorce. Often, when teens ask questions regarding the situation, what they really want to know is how it will affect them directly. Will they have to move and leave their friends and school behind? Will parents expect them to do more household chores? Will there be enough money to live on? Will they be able to choose which parent they want to live with?

When speaking with your teens about your divorce, try to answer their questions openly and honestly. Stick to the facts and keep it simple. Keep in mind that a teen is most likely asking a question because he or she wants to know what the answer will mean to *him or her*. Understanding this should guide your answer.

Just because they are older, teenagers are no more equipped than their younger counterparts to deal with divorce. The news can be equally devastating for all age groups. Make every effort possible to move through your divorce process in ways that will minimize the negative effects on your children. Although a divorce may be inevitable, the manner in which you behave during the divorce is very much in your control.

ALL GROWN UP?

Ironically, child-development experts describe teenagers and toddlers as very similar in behavior and attitude. One would think that the fourteen years between a two-year-old and a sixteen-year-old would result in some degree of maturity, but this is not always the case. The reality is that parents may experience comparable behaviors from both adolescents and their diapered counterparts. Struggles for independence, tantrums, compelling arguments and explanations, the need for control, testing parents' limits, and strong emotions are common occurrences in both groups. However toddler-like a teen's behavior may be at times, there's one thing that teens try hard to convince their parents of: They are already grown up and don't need their parents' assistance (aka "butting in") any longer. However, what teens *say* and what they *mean* are often two very different things.

Many divorcing parents find themselves believing their teens' convincing claims that they are "almost" adults. This is where they can make a big mistake. When they see their kids as adults, they're more likely to share too much with them. Disclosing inappropriate details of a parent's extramarital affair ("You know those business trips Mom has been taking recently? Your mother has been cheating on me and sleeping with her boss for the last six months. We haven't had sex in over two years.") and pulling in the teen as a support ("Oh, God, you know how abusive your father can get. I just can't take his temper anymore. At least he's only slapped you, but now he's punched me in the face.")

are unsuitable options. Such disclosures only give your teen unnecessary anxiety and stress.

Remember that however advanced and experienced your teenager
may seem, he or she is still a child and only just beginning to learn
about adult issues—especially the complexity of love, sex, and romantic relationships. *No teen is ready to hear the inner, sordid details of his or
her parents' sexual liaisons or breakup.*

THE ADOLESCENT'S NEED TO BE LOVED

Although adolescents may push their parents away at every chance,
it's important nonetheless that they know they are loved—*especially*
during a divorce in the family. But by virtue of their advanced age, it
becomes more difficult to show them love like you did when they were
younger. Mommy's or Daddy's kisses, hugs, and snuggles that evoked
gleeful smiles and squeals from a two-year-old may not induce a similar
response from a seventeen-year-old. Especially during the difficult and
often traumatic process of divorce, parents need to be creative about
letting their teens know they care.

Think outside the box to come up with novel, indirect ways to
show your teen you're thinking of him or her. Consider making a bowl
of popcorn (or some other favorite snack) and taking it to your son if he
has been diligently studying for an algebra exam all afternoon. If your
daughter got a new outfit recently, pick up a matching accessory for her
while you're at the mall. You can leave your little gift on her pillow with
a note telling her you were thinking of her. You can make your teen's
favorite dinner unexpectedly one night or perhaps slip on one of his or
her favorite CDs instead of listening to yours when driving together. Or
you could ask to borrow your teen's iPod when you go jogging or you're
mopping the floor. All of these ideas are ways to ensure that your teen
doesn't forget that you care, even when going through difficult times.

Perhaps one of the best ways to show your child that you're making
an effort is with a compliment. Too often, parents of adolescents are critical of their children due to the frequent teenage behaviors and attitudes
that usually annoy adults. Adolescents can be lazy, sarcastic, testy, critical,
and know-it-alls. These undesirable traits often mask the more redeeming qualities (less frequently seen by parents) they may have.

However challenging it may be, try to find the proverbial silver
lining in such things as your child's attitudes and friends. For example,

telling your daughter that her friend has a really cool, unique sense of style is better than asking why her friend can't dress less weird. And if you really do like one of your teen's friends, don't forget to make this clear. In the adolescent time period marked by decreased motivation and lack of energy, it's important to try to find the beauty in it ("Gee, I can remember the days when there was nothing better than staying in bed until 1:00 in the afternoon. Boy, you're lucky—it must be nice to be able to sleep in like that. Enjoy it while you can."). The challenge is whether you can reframe sarcasm, forgetfulness, disorganization, or pessimism into more positive features. Your attempts at viewing the glass as half full rather than as half empty will help you to see your teen in a more favorable light.

Parenting an adolescent is inherently exhausting and tricky. Power struggles, mood swings, defiance, poor decision making, slacking off at school, or alcohol and drug use can be common occurrences in the typical household. This friction between you and your teen can serve a purpose, though; it's the perfect preparation for empowering your offspring to go out on their own. During these trying times, the following point may offer you comfort.

- Your teen will probably not always think it's cool or appropriate to wear some seriously "exposing" trendy fashions, or use the word *dude* in every other sentence.

- You will all survive this difficult period, and most will recuperate relatively unscathed.

- One day your teen will rise before noon and clean up without being asked.

- Take comfort in the fact that your teen will one day have adolescent children of his or her own.

- Remind yourself that you were once seventeen, too.

- Cherish the enjoyable moments with your teen (even if they may seem few and far between!).

QUESTIONS PARENTS SHOULD ASK EACH OTHER

Experts have identified several areas of family life in which divorce affects adolescents. When I bring up these issues in parenting groups, the response is often that parents hadn't thought about these things before they occurred. My motto for divorcing parents with teens is *the devil you know is better than the devil you don't know.* That is, when divorcing parents discuss potential issues and events they may encounter *before* they arise, they create the opportunity to figure out how they'll handle things. This helps them avoid knee-jerk reactions that can be inappropriate or hurtful.

Couples usually don't divorce because they get along well, communicate well, and share the same opinions. Their differences, coupled with the stress and emotional strain that divorce can put on parents, often makes for less-than-stellar responses to problematic issues with teens. Making time to talk with your ex-spouse about issues that relate to your teenager is so important. In fact, in the same way that marriage therapists sometimes "prescribe" that a couple go out on a weekly date without discussing the children, I tell divorcing couples that it is perhaps equally important for them to have a weekly "date," but with the rule that they focus the conversation fully on their children and their children's best interests.

Too often, when parents divorce, each goes his or her own way, so to speak, and loses most contact with the ex-spouse. When this happens, it's fertile ground for teenagers to take full advantage of their parents' lack of connection and communication. Good information exchange between divorced parents equals more supportive parenting.

A good discussion between parents might involve how Mom and Dad would each respond if their teenage son asks to get his nose pierced. Similar questions you might discuss with your ex-husband or ex-wife could include:

- What's an appropriate age for dating? Will you allow your children to have boyfriends or girlfriends in their bedrooms with the door closed?

- If you (the father) have always expected your wife to have the puberty/sexuality talk with your teen daughter, will you be prepared to handle things if your daughter gets her first menstrual period at your house?

- What are your basic expectations with regard to grades, chores, and appropriate language?

- What are the consequences for poor behavior?

- During your parenting time, which of you will follow up on your child's grounding if it is punishment for behaving poorly at the other parent's house?

- How do you feel about phone and going-out curfews?

- What will you do if you find drug paraphernalia in your teen's room?

- How do each of you feel about keeping your teen's secrets from the other parent if the teen requests it?

DIFFERENT RULES FOR DIFFERENT HOUSEHOLDS

Many divorcing parents have huge arguments about the different rules in each of their households. In fact, *rules need not be exactly the same with both parents.* That would be an impossible expectation given that most couples (married or not) disagree at least some of the time on parenting or disciplinary issues.

More important for healthy teen adjustment is *consistency* in rules and expectations, and *supporting the other parent's rules.* Teens want to know the rules and what the consequences will be if they choose not to comply. It only makes life more difficult (for you and your teen) if you punish him or her for coming home past curfew one weekend but let it slide on another occasion.

Likewise, supporting each other's guidelines (assuming the rules are reasonable) is vital. This support helps prevent your teen from attempting to pit you against your ex-spouse. One family I met with for therapy provides a perfect example of the effect of different rules in different households and how a teen can manipulate the situation when parents don't agree.

A fifteen-year-old girl and her mother were having escalating arguments about a 10:00 PM phone curfew the mother imposed on school nights. The daughter claimed that she didn't have a phone curfew at her father's house and that he agreed she didn't need one. Mom countered that it was not appropriate for phone calls to come in and go out at midnight and later. The daughter continued to disobey

Mom's rules and disregard the consequences (i.e., no phone use at all, coming straight home from school, no television). Mom demanded that Dad implement a similar rule at his home on the one night a week the daughter stayed over with him and force her to abide by it. Dad balked at the idea of his ex-wife telling him what to do and how to parent, and the parents became firmly pitted against each other, much to the delight of the daughter, who was getting away with murder.

I asked both parents and the daughter to come to a family session and they reluctantly agreed. In the course of the session I validated both Mom's and Dad's ability and right to parent as they saw fit. I also let them know that both agreeing to the same phone rule seemed highly unlikely and not necessarily their only option. I guided Dad into agreeing that Mom's phone rule was reasonable and appropriate. I then discussed with them the need for the daughter to respect both parents and the rules in each of their homes, even if they were not always the same.

Dad encouraged the daughter to obey the 10:00 PM curfew. "Or what?" the daughter responded sassily. Dad replied with no prompting that he would put a temporary curfew on the phone at his house if he heard the daughter was abusing Mom's rule (much to the dismay of the daughter, who now feared she might not be able to get away with murder any longer).

As teenagers will do, the daughter tested her parents a few times but finally ended up getting off the phone by 10:00 PM at Mom's house while continuing to enjoy later conversations with friends at her Dad's home. Both parents kept their right to parent and neither felt controlled or bossed around by the other. More important, the parental hierarchy remained, both parents felt validated and empowered, and the daughter maintained the more appropriate role as child (rather than as rule maker).

WHO'S THE PARENT HERE?

Teenagers are generally notorious for trying to swap roles with their parents. This can heighten during a divorce, when they attempt to parent their own parents. Many times, a teen will feel the need to "step up to the plate" and become the parent who has moved out. At times this can be helpful, such as when a teenage son begins taking out the garbage and cooking for Mom, or when a daughter helps cut the lawn or cares for and nurtures younger siblings when Dad doesn't have enough time for all their needs. But this teenage assistance can have an unpleasant side as well.

Let's consider the possibility that you or your ex-spouse find a new boyfriend or girlfriend. Some teenagers are *horrified* by the prospect of one of their parents dating or having sexual needs or desires. Your child may be one of those kids who will not hesitate to let you know what they think. Parents have given me many accounts of their teens telling them in no uncertain terms that considering a date would be completely disgusting and unacceptable.

Some teens will try the guilt approach: "It's just not right for you to be considering dating when you have us kids to think about and care for. We need you too much right now to share." Others will go the "attacking the self-esteem" route:

> No offense, Mom [or Dad], but I don't think you should be considering that [dating] at your age. I mean, come on, you're not exactly twenty-one anymore, and things are kind of drooping and all. I don't really think you'd fare well doing the bar scene. You had your time for all that. I just wouldn't want you to try to get all gussied up and end up disappointed 'cause no one's interested.

And then there are those kids who will go for brutal honesty: "That's just downright disgusting that you'd even think about trying to go out on a date! You're a *mother* [or *father*], for God's sake! Gross!"

The bottom line is that a teenager may have strong emotions about a parent's potential dating situation that cause him or her to become judgmental toward this parent. The teen may directly voice his or her negative feelings about Mom or Dad dating or may show it by acting out behaviorally. Sometimes the teen will take on a parenting role in the family. In this instance, the teen may try to set limits with Mom or Dad with regard to his or her dating.

Some teens will go as far as warning their parents' dates, "You'd better not hurt my mom [or dad] or you'll have me to answer to." They may also be jealous or fearful of abandonment. These teens are most likely appalled by the idea of a parent dating as well. After all, think back to your adolescent years. Can you recall feeling completely repulsed by the notion that your parents actually had sex? Most teens fight feverishly to eliminate any such thoughts from their heads. It is only by the harsh and undeniable reality that their parents have indeed produced biological children that teens ever fathom that their mom and dad have any sort of sexual relationship.

Perhaps the best way to deal with this situation is with honesty and by involving the teen in the discussion. You need to maintain your parenting role and refrain from giving too much detail about your adult needs. It's important to acknowledge your teen's attempts at protecting and helping you, rather than just focusing on your annoyance with his or her judgment. Let your teen know you appreciate how he or she feels, but that you need to decide what's important. Avoid lengthy discussions and stick to your decisions. Also, be sure that dating or a new relationship doesn't interfere with or hinder your quality time with your teen.

One family I was seeing for therapy illustrates the parental role-swap during a divorce quite well.

My clients were "Rachel," an almost-divorced mother, and her fourteen-year-old daughter "Jenna." Jenna had been disregarding her mother's attempts at discipline and parenting since the divorce proceedings began nearly six months earlier. Jenna took her anger out primarily on her mother because her mother had gone to court to fight against Jenna living with her father. Rachel fought for her daughter to live with her the majority of the time as well as to limit greatly the time Jenna spent with the father and his girlfriend due to his history of drug use, unemployment, and what Rachel considered a general problem with immoral and risky choices. Rachel decided to seek therapy with her daughter to improve their relationship because they both felt life at home had become unbearable.

One of the biggest fights the mother and daughter repeatedly had was over Jenna's desire to date older boys. An eighteen-year-old senior at the high school she'd be attending the next year had asked her out. Jenna's parents also caught her in several lies about where she had been after school. In one of our first sessions, Jenna admitted to her mother that she had been secretly going out with the eighteen-year-old, against Rachel's wishes. Jenna refused to stop seeing the boy and told her mother she would continue to lie or do whatever she had to do in order to see him because they were in love and were going to get married. At this point Rachel lost her temper and started screaming, "Over my dead body! You cannot just defy me, Jenna! You will stop seeing him or I will ground you indefinitely and I swear to God I'll call the cops if he sets foot near your school or our home!" Jenna was seething. She continued her defiance and stated she didn't care what her mother said.

Rachel regained her cool and went on to explain to her daughter that she feared Jenna was not ready for a romantic relationship with this boy and that Jenna didn't see that she wasn't ready to handle the pressure of sexual intercourse and plans for marriage. Rachel was worried her daughter would get a reputation with other boys as being "easy." This angered Jenna even more. She felt that Rachel saw her as immature. Jenna stated this and then screamed at her mother, "And you're worried about *me* having sex? What about you? You got pregnant with me when you were seventeen and got married at eighteen! You should practice what you preach. And worried about me being a slut? What do you think you are? What about the tube of spermicide I found in your closet a couple of weeks ago? Let's talk about who the slut really is now—and you're not even divorced yet!" Rachel immediately found herself defending the tube of spermicide as being old and left over from when she was still committed to her husband. Furthermore, she insisted she was not dating or having sex with anyone.

The argument had quickly turned to Jenna acting like a parent to her mother and judging her mother's behavior, rather than focusing on the issue at hand—Jenna's misconduct. At this point I interrupted and redirected the session back to the initial conversation.

I then arranged to work with Jenna alone for several weeks to help her express her feelings of anger and disgust about viewing her parents as not only sexual beings, but also as no longer together. We discussed boundaries for respecting Mom's privacy and her right to make adult choices on dating and sex. We also explored ways that Jenna could help her mother feel more comfortable with Jenna's dating in general. This included having the boy over several times so that Rachel could get to know him better before they would make any decision on dating. Jenna agreed not to lie to her mother about her whereabouts. At the next family session, Jenna and Rachel agreed to this arrangement for a period of eight weeks, after which they would discuss how things were going and raise any complaints or concerns they had.

Jenna was soon able to acknowledge her mother's "irrationality" as concern about her. She also realized it would be easier for her and her boyfriend to spend time together at home than to sneak around. Rachel was particularly pleased with the agreement because after the two months were up, Jenna and the eighteen-year-old were no longer seeing each other.

There are countless ways that teens may take on adult responsibilities with their parents, especially when a parent is in a fragile state, which is often the case during divorce. Siding with or defending one parent, directing disappointment or anger toward a parent, and stepping up to protect and care for one parent are just a few of the ways teens may attempt to engage with their parents during a divorce. Any one of these behaviors can create a big problem for the teenager as well as for the parent.

Becoming parental prematurely can interfere with the adolescent's normal developmental task of detaching from parents and becoming more independent. For example, teens in divorcing families sometimes take strong stances against one parent depending on the circumstances of the split. If Dad initiated the divorce and began dating someone else right away, the teen may surmise that Dad was unfaithful, disloyal, and ended the marriage for this other woman. As a result, the teen may refuse to live with or even visit his or her father, thus preventing a natural father–child relationship to progress.

However, the teen may not be making the best choice by emotionally cutting off that parent. He or she may also not choose to live with the parent who could provide the most secure and consistent household. What if by refusing to live with Dad, the teen would spend a great deal of time alone and unsupervised because Mom traveled extensively for business?

Equally as concerning is that this teen may then take on a parental role in order to "take care of" Mom (whom the teen may feel Dad victimized and abandoned). The son or daughter may take on the bulk of the cooking, cleaning, and care for younger siblings. The teen may develop the mind-set that Mom needs him or her, may feel guilty and reluctant to go out with friends or consider college, and may also take on strong fatherly roles with brothers and sisters, including allying with Mom on discipline issues. This can often cause resentment and alienation between the teen and his or her siblings.

It is of utmost importance that, as divorcing parents, you strive to free your teenager from the burden of becoming a parent far before he or she is ready to do so. It's important to push your child gently to go out and enjoy the last years of his or her childhood. You have the responsibility of ensuring your teen that he or she will be okay without your help, although you appreciate the effort.

EXPRESSING FEELINGS

With a disruption or dramatic change to any person's life, a certain amount of adjustment is necessary. Teens are no exception. They need to react to their parents' divorce. Depending on the individual style of each adolescent, this reaction may take the form of anger, sadness, frustration, depression, or complacency.

One mistake divorcing parents frequently make is cutting off a teenager's feelings at every corner, often because the teen is not showing emotion in a calm, respectful, and appropriate manner. Instead, anger or irritation will be their emotional response to the situation.

Everyone needs to release his or her feelings, and parents need to show kids appropriate ways of expressing those feelings. But ask yourself this: What adult going through a trying divorce can claim to have shown only perfect and appropriate expressions of anger, frustration, or sadness? How can we expect our children to do what we as adults are not always capable of? There is simply no one correct way of feeling and behaving when someone is emotional or under stress.

The following scenario is based on a mother and son I counseled. This is an example of how the mom ("Ronnie") was not able to see the need for her adolescent son ("Tyler") to express his anger about and frustration with his parents' volatile separation.

Ronnie brought her sixteen-year-old son, Tyler, to our first therapy session. She was concerned about his escalating anger and acting out at home and at school. He shuffled into the room and sat down in the farthest corner, staring down at his beaten-up sneakers. Clearly he was not thrilled to be meeting with me.

Ronnie spoke first. "Look at the doctor please, Tyler. We're not going to get anywhere unless you participate." I decided to wait a few minutes to observe the interaction between the mom and her son before I interjected anything. Not two seconds after he had made the effort to glance up at me, Ronnie interrupted with, "Wipe that snotty look off your face right now." Tyler grunted under his breath, "Fine!" which was followed by Ronnie asking, "What did you say?" He repeated his response of "Fine!" as she had asked, only this time quite a bit louder. Ronnie responded, "Don't speak to me in that tone!" So he stopped speaking in "that tone" and, in fact, stopped speaking at all. He sat in angry silence.

I had seen enough by now, so I asked Tyler if it was okay for me to ask his mom to leave the room for a few minutes. Before he had a chance to reply, his mother snapped, "Answer her!" Tyler threw his head back and with clenched fists yelled out, "Jesus!" to which Ronnie replied, "Don't you dare use that language!" Tyler could contain his frustration no longer and headed for the door as his mother yelled, "You sit back down right now! Don't you dare leave this room!" At this point, I asked Mom to step outside so I could have the opportunity to explore what was going on with Tyler. Ronnie thankfully agreed.

The first thing I said to Tyler was, "Wow. You must have a lot of reasons to be so angry. What's going on?" Tyler immediately jumped at the chance to express his frustration and talked for the next ten minutes straight. Indeed he had plenty of reason to be upset. Not only were his parents locked in a bitter custody battle, but they asked him to take responsibility for his two younger brothers while Mom worked nights and weekends. He was resentful on many levels, in addition to being very worried about his father. On top of this, his mom had a new boyfriend with whom Tyler didn't get along, and Tyler had to share his room with this man's seventeen-year-old son. Tyler was also experiencing pressure from his teachers due to his falling grades at school.

It was clear to me that both Tyler and his parents were under a great deal of stress. Ronnie and Tyler tended to take their anger out on each other. Not only was Ronnie neglecting to set a good example of coping with stress and anger, but she was also cutting off *all* avenues for Tyler to express his own. Basically, in our session, Tyler could do nothing right as far as his mother was concerned. If he didn't speak, he was uncooperative. If he spoke, the tone was disrespectful and the language was inappropriate. If he looked down, he wasn't paying attention, but if he looked up at me, he wasn't allowed to show any anger. Tyler and his mom were locked in a no-win situation. It took me a few sessions alone with Tyler to hear and begin to understand his pain and frustration.

Future sessions were aimed at bringing Mom and Tyler together to discuss feelings and set limits for acceptable ways of expressing strong emotion. For example, Tyler agreed he would not use profanity or call his mother names when he was angry with her. However, he was allowed to storm off to his room, slam his door, or go down to use the punching bag in the basement. In response to Tyler's resentment about all the extra child-care responsibilities dumped on him, Ronnie agreed to hire a babysitter for one night a weekend so that Tyler could go out with his friends. This was the first time she was also able to acknowledge aloud to Tyler that this situation must be really hard for him. Finally, in order to help Ronnie and her ex-husband learn to set better boundaries with their son and not involve him in their battles, I also did a few intensive parenting sessions with them.

As divorcing parents, you need not be perfect. Being perfect throughout the process of an exhausting and painful divorce only sets unrealistic expectations for your teens about how to handle traumatic events in their own lives. Think about this: Would you want your children to grow up thinking it was not okay to take a personal day off from work or to have a good cry if a failed relationship broke their heart? Would you want your children to feel guilty if they weren't able to get out of bed one morning or failed to fight off the urge for a double-size bowl of Häagen-Dazs after discovering their boyfriend or girlfriend had been cheating on them?

Encourage your teen to express feelings. One way to do this is by sharing your own ways of coping. For instance, sharing that you keep a journal or go running to clear your head is a great disclosure for a teen to hear. Other great examples include asking your teen to join you in meditating, doing yoga, or going out to a movie to "get my mind off things."

Also, refrain from continually saying things like, "It'll all be okay—everything will turn out fine," or, "Maybe you can't see it now, but the divorce is for the best." These encouraging statements may discount what your teen may be feeling. Studies show that a paltry 10 percent of all children experiencing divorce feel relief and positive emotion about the breakup. The other 90 percent may need some help in coping with their negative emotions about the divorce. Don't gloss over your teen's very real feelings. A teen doesn't want to hear that his or her parent doesn't agree, but rather that the parent acknowledges how the teen may be feeling, even if it is in a less-than-positive way.

Sometimes, despite your best efforts, your attempts to get your teen to talk about how he or she feels about the divorce and family changes fails. Your teen may not be able to open up fully simply because you are part of the issue. He or she may not want to worry you or hurt your feelings. If this is the case, try to increase the opportunities your child has with other trusted adult family members and friends. Teachers and coaches may be helpful listeners as well. Encourage your teen to see a therapist if you suspect he or she is experiencing uncharacteristic or unusually strong emotions due to the divorce.

WHEN TO WORRY

I like to use an amusement park bumper car analogy when speaking to parents about when to worry about a teen's mental and emotional health. All human beings are like bumper cars that bump around within a padded arena. They encounter good and bad times and bounce back from each, ending up in a slightly different place each time. Every-thing's okay as long as they stay within the walls of the ride, but if they flip outside the arena due to a traumatic event, things change. They're no longer connected to the ceiling by a metal antenna, and they feel powerless. They're unable to find the energy to get back into the rink and lie hopelessly on the ground instead. They become debilitated and can't see a way out. They don't know where to turn or what to do to get better. *This* is when to worry about your teen.

The National Institute of Health (NIH) reports that an estimated 3 million adolescents, ages 12 to 17, in the United States have had at least one major depressive episode in the last year. However, many theorize the number may be far higher because countless depressed teens remain undiagnosed. Why? Parents, teachers, and other adults who have contact with teenagers may view depressed behaviors as normal adolescent development. People expect moodiness, isolation from the family, and changes in friends.

But if an adult began showing up for work wearing ill-fitting all-black clothing and was increasingly despondent and lethargic, he or she would most likely arouse some attention and concern from fellow employees. People may simply write off the same sudden change in dress and glum mood in a teenager as a fad or an attempt at self-expression.

In recent years, research has uncovered strong evidence that genetics and family history greatly influence the chances of an adolescent developing depression. In fact, having a close family member with a diagnosis of depression makes the teen eleven times more likely to develop it as well.

In addition, changes and stressors (such as a divorce in the family) have the potential to trigger depression in teens. Especially during a time of divorce, as a parent you should remind yourself of the warning signs of depression, as well as consider what you can do to help your teen, who may be suffering from this debilitating illness. With all the turmoil of a divorce, you can miss small symptoms in your child.

Signs of depression in teens are similar to those in adults: significant weight loss or gain, decrease in interest in previously enjoyed hobbies or activities, withdrawal from friends and family, excessive sleeping, increased irritability, constant sadness, a sudden drop in school performance, or expressing a desire to escape one's life.

Many parents are afraid to bring up the possibility of depression with their sons or daughters because they don't want to stir things up further. Their concern is that they may not know what to say or how to state their concern to their children. They hope that the symptoms will eventually just go away. Parents may also simply assume the signs of depression are just part of either normal adolescence or an adjustment to their divorce. Sometimes a parent going through a difficult divorce may just be too consumed with other things to notice the telltale signs.

If you're in doubt about whether your teen's adjustment to the divorce is normal, ask around. Check the Internet for sites on teen depression, ask friends who may have been through this before, call the school, or contact a therapist. Most important, if you suspect your teen is suffering from more than just your average adjustment issues, *have a professional screen your child for depression.*

10

FROM THE MOUTHS OF BABES

At the end of my divorce-parenting class, I show a short video that highlights many of the main concepts we discuss in the class. The difference is that the video is a compilation of real children (not actors) who speak on camera about their experiences with their parents' divorce. This is usually the most powerful part of the class for the participants. Although the children speak about many of the things I had already discussed in the class, it seems to be much more meaningful when the words come directly from their mouths. Perhaps this is because adults have a difficult time slowing their entire world down in order to step back and look at life through their children's eyes.

This entire book is different from others because I have based every bit of it directly on the experiences that children and divorcing parents have shared with me. This final chapter focuses on some of the most common emotional themes that children of divorce experience. It can be helpful for parents to know beforehand how a child may view the divorce, so they can plan how to help support the child accordingly.

STAGES OF GRIEF AND DEATH

Many children mourn the loss of their family as it used to be (before divorce) in a similar way to how they would mourn the death of a loved one. From a child's point of view, something *has* died when his or her parents divorce. The family unit, in the way the child knew it, no longer exists. The child has no say in this decision and must live with the feelings of powerlessness and loss that come along with the parents' decision to terminate their relationship legally.

Some children will say to me, "I miss the way things were so much, I wish I were dead." Obviously, young children are not fully aware of the ramifications of death. However, these types of statements are quite telling as to how children view the magnitude of the loss they experience when their parents divorce. This is especially true if a family falls apart during and after the parents' marriage dissolves.

Elisabeth Kübler-Ross introduced the now-famous pattern of how people grieve in her 1969 book, *On Death and Dying*. Many experts in the field compare her stages of grief (upon a loved one's death) to the stages of grief that children frequently go through when their parents divorce. Many of the children I have seen in therapy for adjustment issues related to their parents' divorce do indeed experience similar stages of grief. Remember that each of the possible stages of grief—denial, anger, bargaining, depression, acceptance—is normal. In time, and if you and your former spouse work hard to avoid behaving poorly during and after the divorce, your children will have a better chance of working through these stages and eventually come to a place of recognition concerning the new make-up of the family unit.

DIFFERENT TIMELINES FOR GRIEF AND ADJUSTMENT

Like any other human being on the planet, each child is unique and will have his or her own specific timeline for grieving the loss of the predivorce family unit. News of divorce will initially devastate some children, and others will barely react at all when their parents tell them they are splitting up. Parents must be patient with their children and understand that each child will need to follow his or her own path of adjustment to the family changes. Even if parents think the child *should be* feeling something more or that the child *should be* acknowledging the improvements in the family since the separation, there is no right or wrong path for children to follow. One example is the story of "Zoe," whom I saw for therapy six years *after* her parents' divorce.

Zoe was a twelve-and-a-half-year-old girl. Her parents referred her for treatment after they reported several months of Zoe's escalating anger toward them and her frequent refusal to go to school. The parents asked me, "Is it really possible that Zoe is upset about our divorce? It happened over six years ago and she never really seemed to have any difficulty adjusting to it before. Why now?"

I needed to meet with Zoe only once to get the answer to her parents' question. Yes, indeed, Zoe had a delayed (negative) reaction to her parents' divorce. As she poured her heart out to me, complete with angry words and tears, it was clear that Zoe had good reason to feel the way she did.

When Zoe was six and a half years old, her parents divorced in a fairly amicable fashion. Zoe had just begun the first grade in a wonderful, warm, small school. She loved her teacher, won awards, and had lots of little friends with whom she would congregate regularly both on the playground and after school. After the divorce, the family had to sell the house, give three cats to a neighbor, and both parents moved; Dad rented a small apartment in a three-family house and Mom relocated to a nearby city where she and Zoe shared a two-bedroom apartment.

Zoe began second grade at a much larger school in a city atmosphere. She was initially afraid to go on the bus because the kids were "really big and bossy and loud." After a while, it appeared to Zoe's parents that she had successfully blended into the school system and seemed to be doing well. However, this was not the experience that Zoe recalled.

"I never fit into that new school system," Zoe vented to me. "No one ever paid attention to me there, and it is still that way today—I'm a nobody. I'm not popular like I was at my old school and barely have any friends at all now. I didn't get asked to the dance this month and the teachers all hate my work. I hate my life here. My parents were so effing selfish when they got divorced. No one ever thought about me or how I would feel about a new school. If they had never gotten divorced, we'd still be in our old house, not this stupid apartment with peeling walls, and I'd be doing well in school and have my old friends back. This is their entire effing fault!"

When I met with Zoe's parents after asking her permission to do so, I was able to help her parents understand the root of Zoe's anger. Zoe's mom asked, "But why now? She never seemed to complain in third or fourth grade about all this." My answer to her was simple: "If we look at the developmental stages, fifth and sixth grade are very important times for social involvement. Perhaps when Zoe was eight or nine or ten, not feeling popular or as well liked wasn't such a big deal, but when grades and dances and such begin to become important, suddenly Zoe feels left out. When a child is young and she has a bad day at school, a hug from Daddy or baking cookies with Mommy can ease the pain. But when a child is older, no amount of hugs or cookie batter can stop the sting of not fitting in socially with your peers."

As with Zoe, not all children follow any one specific path of healing from a divorce. Sometimes, the effects can linger for years and resurface at another stage of life. *Be sensitive to your child's individuality and try not to hold him or her to your own personal standards for grieving and moving on.*

THE LITTLE THINGS COUNT

Similar to how differently each child heals from a divorce in the family, all children have unique experiences that force them to face the stark new reality of the changes in their families. Most divorcing parents agree that they don't think, "Wow, it's really over," when they sign the final divorce papers. For some parents, reality sinks in when they are picked up at a bar for the first time after the divorce and realize, "Oh my gosh, I can really do this if I want to—I'm a single person now."

Likewise, there are a variety of different moments in which a child will confront the recognition of the divorce being real. Like the young boy who burst into tears one morning after seeing one gaping, empty black hole in the four-holed toothbrush holder where his dad's toothbrush used to fit, children have shared many of these "realization moments" with me over the years. Children can use all five senses when they experience the family changes—certain sights, smells, and sounds are especially poignant losses for children. One young girl described feeling like she was "punched in the gut" when she went into her mom's closet and it was only half full because "Dad had moved all his clothes out." Another boy stated, "Our house is so empty with some of the furniture gone from it." One child told me that although he personally hated Cocoa Puffs cereal, he missed the chocolaty smell of it in the pantry because it was always there when his dad was living there. Another child complained that he couldn't fall asleep very easily now because he missed the muffled drone of the television on downstairs when his dad lived there. Another boy said he always used to wake up automatically for school each morning because he'd hear his mom's blow-dryer running. "Now," he says, "I have to use an alarm clock to get up or I'll sleep in and be late for the bus."

Unfortunately, as much as you want to fix things for your children, the process each child goes through is his or her own; the child has to go through the experience at his or her own natural speed. You can support your children during these difficult moments by being gentle with them and tolerant of strong emotions or anger for a short while after the reality of the predivorce family loss sinks in. Sometimes, sharing your own moment of realization with the child can comfort him or her greatly. One mom I had in counseling told her young son that her moment of realization came when "I skipped the entire frozen food aisle at the grocery store one day because I didn't have to buy all the vegetarian frozen entrees and special waffles your dad always wanted in the house."

THINGS THAT HURT KIDS MOST

Although experts write frequently about which parental behaviors harm children most, I am always quite interested in what the *children themselves* tell me is most hurtful. The following are some comments from children on what most upset them during their parents' divorce.

"They just fight all the time and I just want to run away when they do. I hate to hear them fighting."
This is perhaps the most frequent complaint I hear from children. The exchange of angry, heated words has a big impact on children. Kids tell me all the time that hearing their parents fight "makes me feel like I'm going to throw up" or "It [the fighting] makes my heart hurt." During a trying and often stressful time such as divorce, parents are more likely to spar with each other. I cannot stress how important it is for divorcing parents to keep their arguments away from the children. Hearing these feuds gives children a great deal of unnecessary pain.

"My mom always tries to tell me that my dad is trying to get me away from her so I won't ever see her anymore. It makes me scared to think about that."
The mom in this scenario thought she was doing the right thing in telling her son that the dad was trying to take him away from her.

This was, in fact, the mom's belief about the dad's intent, and perhaps it may have been the dad's true intent as well. But the only thing the mom succeeded in doing in this case was to transfer her own fears onto her young son, who did not know what to do with the anxiety this knowledge provoked in him. Additionally, instead of the response she had hoped for from the son (distancing from Dad), the mom noticed that her plan had backfired. The son did not pull away from the dad; rather he gravitated toward the dad in an attempt to keep him happy so he wouldn't get mad and "steal me away from my mom."

"My dad tells me to tell my mom stuff when I go home to her house."

Children should not be the messengers between divorced parents. This can cause unnecessary stress for children when they are trying to remember the things they were supposed to report to the other parent. In addition, parents should not burden children with worry about the underlying messages they think they are carrying to the other parent. A child may interpret "Ask your father whether he sent the child support payment yet," as "You're late again with the child support money and we can never count on you for anything."

The father of a nine-year-old girl I saw for therapy asked her to tell her mom to give back his tool kit so he could fix the girl's various toys and put up some outside summer recreational equipment. The girl came into our session, told me about her father's request, and then said, "So I just keep telling him [the dad] I forgot to ask Mom for the tool kit because I didn't want to ask her and then she'd get mad. I told my dad I didn't need any of my toys fixed anyway—I don't really even play with those anymore." I found out later that the girl did indeed still play with her toys and swing set outside but that her fear of angering Mom was enough for her to sacrifice her own objects of enjoyment in order to smooth over her parents' rift about the tools.

"Stop saying mean things about Mom. It makes me feel bad, even if I know the things you're saying about her are true."

Nobody likes to feel bad, and children are no different. Sometimes it is easier just to avoid having to acknowledge painful things about a parent than it is to have to face it during a fragile time like divorce. When one parent says bad things about the other, the child hears the hurtful facts. A child will, in his or her own time, figure out each parent and decide which parent(s) is deserving of the child's affections, involvement, and trust—*regardless of whether the other parent insisted on trying to prepare the child beforehand with all the details of what a jerk the other parent is.*

"It hurts me when you hurt Mom."

What many divorcing parents forget is that when they disparage or intentionally hurt the other parent, they often hurt the child as well. For example, a dad may yell at the mom outside in the driveway after he's dropped off the kids. He thinks they don't hear him because they're inside and he isn't yelling at them, so he believes he is doing no harm to the children. In fact, the children are up in the bedroom watching them fight, and one child in particular is feeling very sad that Daddy is yelling at Mommy. *Saying hurtful things to the other parent hurts the children as well.*

"I wish he [my dad] wouldn't get mad when I tell my mom stuff about my visits with him. Why should I have to keep secrets? I should be able to talk about what happened if I want, you know, because it's my life too."

You've got to admit it—this kid makes a lot of sense. Why shouldn't a child be able to share good and bad events that happened in his or her life that day while spending time with the other parent? One parent I saw for therapy said to her son, "You told Dad about our weekend together. Why'd you have to say anything? Now Dad is mad at me!" A parent should not expect a child to keep his or her "two lives" completely separate after divorce. However, if the child seems to be sharing details with the other parent for a spiteful or manipulative purpose, the parent might say, "You know, I don't feel like I have any privacy when you go and tell Mom everything I do and say. We are divorced now and we don't have to share every little thing anymore. I'd appreciate it if you left our business together here instead of taking it all home to Mom."

"This is not fair."

Some parents like to respond with the old adage "Oh, well, life's not fair," when a child says, "It's not fair." When a divorce happens, it is better for parents to acknowledge that many things about what's happening in the family are indeed not going to seem fair. You might even want to list a few complaints of your own. This validates the child's feelings rather than trying to convince him or her otherwise.

"I'm never going to my dad's house again unless he gives me a later bedtime."

Children have mixed emotions about all the changes they must adapt to when their parents divorce. Having different rules at each of the two homes can prove frustrating for the child and serve as a golden opportunity for the child to manipulate the situation.

Not liking a bedtime is not an adequate reason for spending less time with Dad. If the parents were married and in the same home, this would not be an issue. Mom needs to support the child going to Dad's house even if the child doesn't like the rules there. Mom may also help the child practice appropriate communication with the parent about his or her concern with the bedtime and also help the child deal with disappointment in a calm manner if certain rules are simply nonnegotiable.

"The only person who understands me is Mr. Keith, my math teacher."

Many divorcing parents feel hurt when their child makes this type of comment. However, it is sometimes impossible for a child to open up fully to a parent, no matter how competent that parent may be, simply because the parent is part of the problem—the divorce. During and after a divorce, parents must still parent the child and do not have the luxury that outsiders (like Mr. Keith) often do; those outside of the immediate family have a certain disconnect from the situation and can offer support, a no-strings-attached shoulder to cry on, or helpful suggestions for how to relate to a parent or what to do to escape the situation at home if it becomes overwhelming.

As long as the parents know and trust Mr. Keith and monitor their child's time spent with him, it may be a good thing the child feels heard and understood by someone during this difficult time. The parents should speak with Mr. Keith privately to keep the lines of communication open. A child frequently thinks that his or her parents do not understand, no matter how hard they try, because if they really did understand, *they wouldn't get a divorce.*

"I hate when Mommy cries."

Crying, among many other emotional expressions, is a common and appropriate occurrence during the divorce process. Indeed, there are often things to cry about. When children are uncomfortable with a parent's crying, it is usually because the child's understanding of crying is that it happens out of hurt and sadness and, therefore, the child's empathic side kicks in and the child wants to help the parent feel better. A parent need not avoid crying in front of a child on occasion; it is an important part of the grieving process that the parent does not need to mask in order to protect the child. However, the parent should be sure to let the child know that crying can be a good thing and that it doesn't always need to be fixed. A cautionary note: If a parent is suffering from depression that includes serious, frequent bouts of crying, the parent needs to seek professional help as soon as possible to prevent the child from assuming a caretaking role.

"I wish they [my parents] would stop asking me to talk to them. I just don't want to talk about it right now."

Like every other person in the universe, a child may sometimes not feel like talking about "it." A divorce is a life-changing event and one that often causes a great deal of sadness, anger, and confusion for a child. Emotions may be difficult to talk about. Parents need not push their children to speak about how they are feeling according to the parents' timetable. Each child will have his or her own grieving path to follow and each will need to process and talk about the divorce and family changes in different ways. However, if a parent is concerned that a child is hoarding his or her feelings inside and not talking at all about the divorce to anyone, it may be wise to have the child talk to a professional (e.g., a therapist or a school guidance counselor) who is trained to look for and deal with a child's coping mechanisms.

"I hate Mommy."

Hate is a strong word and many parents cringe at the sound of it, especially when that word is used to describe how the child feels about one of his or her parents. A parent should not deny the child's feelings by telling the child he or she must never use the word, nor should the parent encourage its use. It is best to say something like, "I know you are feeling really angry with Mommy right now. We all feel that way sometimes." Then, the parent can help the child talk about what it would take for the child to feel differently about the parent he or she "hates." Some parents also choose to discuss forgiveness with their child or encourage the child to talk about why he or she feels this way. All of these ideas validate the child's feeling while simultaneously encouraging solution-oriented talk.

"I can't go with Daddy because Mommy needs me."
Children often create an image of one parent as the needier of the two when a divorce occurs. The child then develops a personal mission of protecting and caring for that needy parent. The parent to whom the child clings should not reinforce this setup by saying things like, "He doesn't want to go with you. He would rather stay with me." Rather, the parent should encourage the child to go with the other parent by saying things such as, "Go with Daddy—you haven't seen him in a while and I'm sure you'll have fun. I'll be fine, honey. I have lots of things to do to keep me busy." It's important that parents send the message of "I want and enjoy you" rather than "I need you" to their children.

COMMON QUESTIONS CHILDREN ASK
(AND SOME SIMPLE RESPONSES)

Children ask many questions during and after a divorce. Some of these questions take parents by surprise, and they are often uncertain how to answer them. The following are a few tough questions children have asked in my sessions and some simple, direct ways for parents to respond. These responses are general and intended to be basic suggestions. Parents should consider the child's age and modify their responses to address the specific situation. There is no one right way to answer a child's questions. However, the following suggestions are good starting points for parents who are struggling with what to say to their kids.

"Will I have a new mommy or daddy?"
"After the divorce, many new people may come into your life who care about you very much. Only you can decide what kind of a relationship you will have with each of them and what you feel comfortable calling them, but no matter what, you will always have one mommy and daddy. That will never change."

"Why don't I see my cousin Rachel anymore?"
If it's because of the parenting plan arrangement, an appropriate answer might be: "Sometimes after a divorce, because the kids don't always see each parent all the time and on every holiday, the kids see less of certain family members, too. Maybe we can talk to Dad about getting you together with Rachel sometime soon."

If it's because a family member has "taken sides" against one parent and refuses to see that parent, a fitting response might be: "Sometimes a divorce can bring up strong feelings and opinions for other family members, and their anger or hurt makes them want a little space from the family. We'll just have to wait and see what happens and we'll try to talk to her later when she's had some time to think about things."

"Will Daddy love his new children more than me?"

"We all have enough room in our hearts to love many, many people, right? [*You can also list all the people the child loves, including pets, at this point.*] Daddy will never run out of love for you no matter how many children he has. Parents don't ever love any one child less than another—parents love each child differently. And you will always be your father's first child. That can never change, and in a special way, you taught him a lot about what he knows about parenting. You were the first person to show him what love between a child and a parent is all about."

"If I promise to be really good, will you get back together?"

"All kids show good and bad behavior sometimes. Being good or not good is not ever the reason parents get divorced. So, no, if you change your behavior, it won't mean that we will get back together. So just keep being you, exactly like you are, because that's who we love so much, no matter what."

"Do I have to like Mom's new boyfriend?"

"Of course we can't *make* you like someone, but we would like for you to give Mom's new boyfriend a chance. It would be easier for everyone if it turned out that you liked him, even just a little bit, because he will be spending a lot of time with the family."

"Why can't the dog come back and forth with me to Mom's and Dad's?"

"I know you miss Rocco [the dog] when you're at Mom's [or Dad's] house, but we decided it was too difficult to cart Rocco back and forth between the two houses. Also, Dad's house is better equipped for Rocco; it has a fenced-in yard and carpeted floors so he doesn't slip and slide around."

"But if Dad lets me do it, why can't you?"

"People are different and parents are different, too. I know it's hard to get used to following two sets of rules at the two different homes, but that's just the way it is going to be. Just because Dad lets you do it isn't a good enough reason for me to feel comfortable letting you do it."

"Do you still love Daddy?"

"No, I don't love Daddy the way I used to. It takes a very special kind of love to make a marriage last. It doesn't work the same way that always loving your child works."

Another response might be: "Of course I still love Daddy but not in the way I used to. There are many different kinds of love, and the kind you need to make a marriage work, we don't have anymore."

"Why did Mommy leave us?"

"Mommy didn't leave *us*. Mommy left the house. Mommy left the marriage. But Mommy did not, and will not, ever leave *you*."

"When will Dad stop acting like a jerk?"

"I can't answer that. I don't know why your dad says and does certain things. I can't speak for your dad, but I think that if you feel that strongly about how he is acting, it's important for you to talk to him about it."

"Why do you hate Mommy so much?"

"I don't hate Mommy. I get angry with her, yes. But I have gotten angry at many people in my life and not hated them. Your mom is a great person in a lot of ways and there are things I like about her very much. But Mommy and I are disagreeing about lots of things right now and sometimes we get frustrated and mad at each other. We'll work it all out, though."

"Why are you and Mom getting a divorce?"

"There are many reasons your mom and I are getting divorced. Lots of the reasons you will not be able to understand until you are older. There are lots of things that Mom and I disagree on, and these things are so important that neither one of us can give up what we think and feel. I know it's confusing to you now, but we'll keep talking about it and one day when you're older you might be able to understand it all a little bit better."

AFTERWORD

No doubt, divorce is disruptive and painful, but it doesn't have to be destructive. Human beings, including the youngest victims of divorce (the children), are wired to adapt to new environments and adjust to significant life changes. However, as this book highlights, there are many things parents do to make the experience of divorce far worse than it has to be.

If there is one thing divorcing parents have in common, it is the love and concern for the well-being of their children. As you move through the difficult process of divorce and afterward, let your children be your guiding light. Before making any move, think about how your actions will affect your child's well-being and feelings. You have far more power than you will ever know.

Appendix A:
Resources for
Divorcing Parents

RESOURCES FOR ALL DIVORCING PARENTS

Books

Ahrons, Constance. *The Good Divorce: Keeping Your Family Together When Your Marriage Comes Apart.* New York: Harper Paperbacks, 1994.

Botwinick, Amy. *Congratulations on Your Divorce: The Road to Finding Your Happily Ever After.* Deerfield Beach, FL: Health Communications, 2005.

Doskow, Emily. *Nolo's Essential Guide to Divorce.* Berkeley, CA: Nolo Publishing, 2006.

LaCrosse, Robert E. and Christine A. Coates. *Learning from Divorce: How to Take Responsibility, Stop the Blame, Move On.* San Francisco: Jossey-Bass, 2003.

Moskovitch, Deborah. *The Smart Divorce: Proven Strategies and Valuable Advice from 100 Top Divorce Lawyers, Financial Advisors, Counselors, and Other Experts.* Chicago: Chicago Review Press, 2007.

Sember, Brette McWhorter. *The Divorce Organizer and Planner.* New York: McGraw-Hill, 2004.

Trafford, Abigail. *Crazy Time: Surviving Divorce and Building a New Life.* New York: Harper Perennial, 1992.

Ventura, John and Mary Reed. *Divorce for Dummies.* Hoboken, NJ: Wiley, 2005.

Websites
www.divorce360.com
www.DivorceHQ.com
www.DivorceLinks.com
www.DivorceMag.com
www.divorcenet.com
www.DivorceRecovery101.com
www.divorcesource.com
www.DivorceSupport.com
www.SmartDivorce.com
www.ourfamilywizard.com
www.divorceandteens.weebly.com

RESOURCES FOR DIVORCING DADS

Books

Baker, Simon and Alley Einstein. *How to Be a Great Divorced Dad.* Berkshire, England: Foulsham, 2007.

Davies, Steve. *The Divorced Dad's Handbook: Practical Advice and Guidance for All Fathers During Divorce or Separation.* Oxford, England: How-to Books, 2007.

Fouquet, C. Stephen. *Divorced Dads: Real Stories of Facing the Challenge.* Minneapolis: Fairview Press, 1996.

Knox, David and Kermit Leggett. *The Divorced Dad's Survival Book: How to Stay Connected with Your Kids.* Cambridge, MA: Da Capo Press, 2000.

Mandelstein, Paul. (2006). *Always Dad: Being a Great Father During and After Divorce.* Berkeley, CA: Nolo Publishing, 2006.

McClure, F. Daniel and Jerry B. Saffer. *Wednesday Evenings and Every Other Weekend: From Divorced Dad to Competent Co-Parent: A Guide for the Non-Custodial Father.* Charlottesville, VA: Van Doren Company, 2001.

Shimberg, Elaine F. and Michael Shimberg. *The Complete Single Father: Reassuring Answers to Your Most Challenging Situations.* Cincinnati: Adams Media Corporation, 2007.

Thomas, Nick. *Dating After Divorce for The Single Daddy: How to Date Successfully After Divorce.* Create Space Publishing, 2015.

Websites
www.about.com (keywords: divorced dads)
www.DadsDivorce.com
www.divorcedfathers.com
www.Divorceinfo.com
www.fatherville.com
www.fightforyourkids.com
www.nolo.com

RESOURCES FOR DIVORCING MOMS

Books
Colopy, Elsa. *The Single Mom's Guide to Finding Joy in the Chaos.* Grand Rapids, MI: Revell Books, 2006.

Engber, Andrea and Leah Klungness. *The Complete Single Mother: Reassuring Answers to Your Most Challenging Concerns.* Avon, MA: Adams Media Corporation, 2006.

Ferber, Donna. *From Ex-Wife to Exceptional Life: A Woman's Journey Through Divorce.* Farmington, CT: Purple Lotus Press, 2005.

Kahn, Sandra. *Leaving Him Behind: Cutting the Cord and Breaking Free After the Marriage Ends.* New York: Ballantine Books, 1992.

Karst, Patrice. *The Single Mother's Survival Guide.* Freedom, CA: Crossing Press, 2000.

Miller, Holiday and Shepherd, Valerie. T*he Ex-Wives' Guide to Divorce: How to Navigate Everything from Heartache and Finances to Child Custody.* New York: Skyhorse Publishing, 2016.

Moffett, Kay and Sarah Touborg. *Not Your Mother's Divorce: A Practical Girlfriend-to-Girlfriend Guide to Surviving the End of an Early Marriage.* New York: Broadway Books, 2003.

Simpson, Bria. *The Balanced Mom: Raising Your Kids Without Losing Your Self.* Oakland, CA: New Harbinger Publications, 2006.

Sweet, Rose. *A Woman's Guide to Healing the Heartbreak of Divorce.* Peabody, MA: Hendrickson Publishers, 2001.

Websites
www.CafeMom.com
www.divmomsclub.com
www.divorce360.com (keywords: divorced moms)
www.singlemothers.org
www.SingleRose.com
www.WomansDivorce.com

RESOURCES FOR GAY PARENTS

Books
Sember, Brette McWhorter. *The Complete Gay Divorce*. Franklin Lakes, NJ: Career Press, 2006.

Websites
www.DailyStrength.org
www.divorcenet.com (keywords: gay and lesbian parents)

RESOURCES FOR DIVORCED PARENTS WHO BEGIN DATING AGAIN

Books
Bartlett, Joshua. *Dating After Divorce: The Essential Guide That Will Help You Make The Right Decision*. Learning Life E-Books, 2011.

Ellison, Sheila. *The Courage to Love Again: Creating Happy, Healthy Relationships After Divorce*. San Francisco: HarperOne, 2002.

Frisbee, David. *Dating After Divorce*. Beacon Hill Press, 2012.

Gray, John. *Mars and Venus Starting Over: A Practical Guide for Finding Love Again After a Painful Breakup, Divorce, or the Loss of a Loved One*. New York: Harper Paperbacks, 1998.

Hartman, Christie. *Dating the Divorced Man: Sort Through the Baggage to Decide if He's Right for You*. Avon, MA: Adams Media Corporation, 2007.

McKenna, Sharon. *Sex and the Single Mom: The Essential Guide to Dating, Mating, and Relating*. Berkeley, CA: Ten Speed Press, 2006.

Sarah, Rachel. *Single Mom Seeking: Playdates, Blind Dates and Other Dispatches from the Dating World*. Emeryville, CA: Seal Press, 2006.

Schneider, Meg F. and Martine Myer. *Sex and the Single Parent: A Guide for Parents Who Find Themselves Back in the Dating Game.* New York: Perigee Trade, 2002.

Tessina, Tina. *The Unofficial Guide to Dating Again.* Hoboken, NJ: Wiley, 1999.

Websites
www.DivorcedPeopleMeet.com
www.ParentsAlready.com
www.SingleParentMeet.com
www.suite101.com

RESOURCES FOR DIVORCING PARENTS EXPERIENCING A HIGH-CONFLICT RELATIONSHIP WITH AN EX-SPOUSE

Books
Garrity, Carla and Mitchell Baris. *Caught in the Middle: Protecting the Children of High-Conflict Divorce.* New York: Lexington Books, 1994.

Ross, Julie and Judy Corcoran. *Joint Custody with a Jerk: Raising a Child with an Uncooperative Ex.* New York: St. Martin's Griffin Press, 1996.

Thayer, Elizabeth and Jeffrey Zimmerman. *The Co-Parenting Survival Guide: Letting Go of Conflict After a Difficult Divorce.* Oakland, CA: New Harbinger Publications, 2001.

Warshak, Richard. *Divorce Poison: Protecting the Parent-Child Bond from a Vindictive Ex.* New York: ReganBooks, 2001.

RESOURCES TO FIND A SKILLED PROVIDER IN SEPARATION AND DIVORCE

The Association of Family and Conciliation Courts website (www.afccnet. org) is dedicated to its interdisciplinary nationwide members including judges, social workers, parent educators, and custody evaluators.

The American Academy of Matrimonial Lawyers website (www. aaml.org) contains information and nationwide contacts for family lawyers, divorce attorneys, marriage annulment, and child custody.

The American Association for Marriage and Family Therapy website (www.aamft.org) contains information and contact data for licensed marriage and family therapists nationwide.

Appendix B:
Common Mistakes
Divorcing Parents
Make

See chapters 3 and 6 for more information about the topics in this list.

1. *Ending the Marriage Too Quickly.* Are you really sure it's over? Did the decision to divorce come from a moment of emotional exhaustion?
2. *Criticizing the Other Parent in Front of the Children.* This also includes saying bad things about your ex-spouse to people who may repeat them back to your children, leaving nasty messages that your children may hear or overhear, or engaging in malicious Internet blogging.
3. *Fighting in Front of the Children.* This involves verbal fighting but also includes sarcasm and physical fighting.
4. *Making Erroneous Assumptions.* Is your child embellishing? Are you assuming your ex-spouse has abilities now that he or she did not have before the divorce?
5. *Completely Cutting Off from a Child.* No relationship at all with a parent unless there is significant risk of abuse or neglect is not healthy for a child.
6. *Using the Wrong Words.* "You are acting just like your mother [father]" may be hurtful words to a child whose parents are going through a divorce.

7. *Using the Child as an Informant or a Spy.* Children need to be left out of the middle of their parents' issues during a divorce and should never be expected to channel information to one parent about the other.
8. *Using the Child as a Confidante.* Children need to be children, not friends or supports for their parents during divorce.
9. *Forcing Children to Choose Sides.* A child should not have to "choose sides" in a divorce. Rather, the child should know he or she simply has *two* parents who love him or her.
10. *Failing to Be Consistent in Payment of Child Support.* Not sticking to an agreed-upon payment plan can cause suffering for both the parents and the child.
11. *Giving in to Children's Manipulation.* Divorce can sometimes make it easy for children to manipulate parents.
12. *Failing to Follow Through with Agreed-Upon Pickups and Drop-Offs.* Not only can poor follow-through in this area cause worry and angst for a parent, but it also sets a poor example for children on respecting others' time.
13. *Not Taking Care of Yourself.* Perhaps the most important thing you can do for your child during the trying times of divorce is taking care of yourself. A healthy parent is a better parent.

Acknowledgments

Many thanks to all the divorcing parents and their children with whom I have worked over the years; it is only through your shared experiences and struggles that I could write this book. Kudos to all these parents who have gone "above and beyond" in order to ensure the security and comfort of their children during this difficult time—M.M., you're a great dad! I want to also acknowledge all the parents I've worked with who were on the brink of divorce but worked extraordinarily hard to save their marriages, much to the delight of their children, especially J.S., your dedication and selflessness are truly remarkable. You set the bar high for parents; I am honored to count you as my friend!

Thank you to all the professionals in the field who supported the idea for this guide, recognized the importance of working together in the best interests of the children and gave feedback along the way, especially attorney, social worker extraordinaire, and dear friend Dina Menchetti, and the "queen" in this arena, Michele Weiner Davis, you are my inspiration, lovely lady!

Thank you to the first literary agent who expressed such support and need for this book and pointed me in the right direction, Susan Schulman, and to the second, Tracy Howell, who passed away unexpectedly before being able to guide this book to publication. Thank you also to Michael Vaughn for your initial editing assistance.

A most heartfelt thank-you to my current agent and friend, Regina Ryan, who worked tirelessly to find the perfect "home" for my work and for time and effort she spent editing and helping me focus my proposal. I'd also like to acknowledge and thank Bob Nirkind, who improved the manuscript through tireless editing and excellent suggestions. We were a productive writing-editing team. Thanks for making my first time through the process so easy and enjoyable!

Thanks to the entire team at Skyhorse Publishing, especially to Joseph Sverchek, for such wonderful support and for believing in this book. It has been an honor and pleasure to publish with you. To Brooke Rockwell, so grateful to have you join us this time around.

Many, many thanks to my friend and colleague, Alana, for sharing the journey, making me laugh, and for your tech-savvy at the eleventh hour manuscript assistance. I am indebted! To Bob, thanks for having my back and being the best guide a newbie could ask for—I will miss you more than you could ever know. Jerry and Hassan, thank you for rounding out the awesome crew! Love you all.

To J.S., M.M., and RJ, thanks for showing me so much I didn't know the first time around. And especially to C.B., you are where it all started—I am forever grateful.

To S.C., there are no words to describe the gratitude I have for you, and the innumerable ways you have helped me. You are (and always have been) the very best teacher. I can only hope I am lucky enough to get another thirty years out of you. Much love!

Lastly, but as always most importantly, thank you to my three beautiful daughters for bearing with me as I wrote and researched for innumerable hours on yet another book idea. You are my rewards every day of my life—I love you!

About the Author

Lisa René Reynolds is a therapist in private practice, specializing in marriage counseling and therapy with families going through divorce. She has master's and PhD degrees in marital and family therapy, and she is dual-licensed in Connecticut and New York State. In addition, Lisa is assistant professor and director of the Marriage and Family Therapy Graduate Program at Iona College, just ouside of New York City. She has written several professional journal, mainstream magazine, and newspaper articles. Her past nonfiction books include *Coming Out and Covering Up: Catholic Priests Talk About the Sex Scandals in the Church* (Dead End Street Press, 2004; foreword by Andrew M. Greeley). Her fiction work, *Who Holds the Torch for Eddie?*, on the eerie and infamous (Edgar Allan) Poe Toaster ritual is available as an e-book through barnesandnoble.com and kobobooks.com.

INDEX